GRACE LIVINGSTON HILL

Grace in her study, about 1930.

Grace Livingston Hill

ROBERT MUNCE

Tyndale House Publishers, Inc.
WHEATON, ILLINOIS

First printing, April 1986
Library of Congress Catalog Card Number 85-52213
ISBN 0-8423-1179-3
Copyright © 1986 by Robert L. Munce
All rights reserved
Printed in the United States of America

To my wife
MARTI
*who encouraged me
to write this book
and to my mother*
RUTH LIVINGSTON HILL MUNCE

*who contributed
to its contents
and assisted
in the proofreading.*

*This dedication
is also to the
many admirers of
Grace Livingston Hill
who have wanted
to know more
about her personal life.
It is my prayer
that they will be
inspired by her life
and
pointed once again
to the God
she served.*

CONTENTS

INTRODUCTION

W H O !

With apologies to an old poet.

Who is it's always in the way?
  And never has enough to pay?
    And always has too much to say?
                              My mother-in-law!

Who is it wears such worldly clothes?
  And won't put powder on her nose?
    And when I ask her never goes!
                              My mother-in-law!

Who goes to banquets in my stead,
  And leaves me home to eat dry bread,
    And go quite early to my bed?
                              My mother-in-law!

Who is it frustrates all my plans?
   From Garden Plots to Traveling Vans?
      And all I say she straightway cans?
                              My mother-in-law!

Who argues long and out to win
   Of doggies, or the point of a pin?
      And counts all fun a doggone sin?
                              My mother-in-law!

Who chases Herb from early morn,
   And sends him out upon the lawn,
      And hates the Reo all forlorn?
                              My mother-in-law!

Who laughs at me when I am cross?
   And tries to be an awful boss?
      And never makes enough hard sauce?
                              My mother-in-law!

THE WRITER thrust back her chair and laughed out loud to herself. Then she added the final touch. She signed her name in the well-taught hand of her generation, a fine legible script: *Grace Livingston Hill.*

The signature was a fine touch of humor: The renowned novelist writing a "not-so-hot" poem about herself, and then signing her well-known name.

The poem was received several days later by her son-in-law, Wendell, who enjoyed reading it to his wife, who broke into titillating peals of laughter. The poem was accompanied by a lovely warmhearted letter that only a loving member of one's family could write.

This was the essence of Grace Livingston Hill. A lover of life, a lover of her family and other people, but above all a lover of the Lord Jesus, the Son of God, and Sovereign of her life. Living with the King in her life kept her happy and humble for she realized who had granted, as a gift, her success.

Life for Grace was full of joy and sadness, as it is for everyone, but she had unshakable faith in the rightness of God's ways, and she shared that faith with others.

In 1899, at the age of thirty-four, Grace lost both her husband and her father. Facing the need to move (the family lived in a manse provided by the church where her husband had been pastor) and to support two young girls and a mother would have crushed most women. But with faith and fortitude, as well as her good sense of humor, Grace provided a home and a living for her family. This was the woman who was later referred to by her publisher as "America's most beloved author!"

ALL THROUGH THE NIGHT

CHAPTER I

THE SOUTH was losing the Civil War. It had fielded a strong army, and had great generals. Its land produced excellent crops and the supply lines were, for the most part, adequate. What was lacking was obvious. It had no industrial base to build and maintain a war machine, and almost no navy to keep harbors open so that needed war materials could be imported.

As soon as the war was inevitable, the North surrounded every supply line, and by April of 1861 the Yankee navy had fully blockaded every southern port. The northern fleet numbered less than 150 ships at the outset of the war, and not all of these were ready for service. With swift decision and typical energy the Northerners updated their fleet of ships and riverboats, protecting many with bullet-proof iron sheets. The fleet grew to nearly 700 vessels by 1865, with 150 of these blocking Charleston and Wilmington harbors alone. With supplies cut off, the South could not maintain itself on the battlefield.

On April 9, 1865, the war was over. People sighed and hoped that some of the suffering would end. Then only five days later, on April 14, 1865, President Abraham Lincoln was shot. He died the following day.

Two years earlier, when the war was at its height, Marcia Livingston gave birth to a son. Her pastor-husband, Rev. Charles Livingston, was at her side. All seemed well at the time, but during the following day the baby had trouble breathing and, although the doctor did all that he could, the child died.

Charles comforted his wife with tender words and with promises from God's Word, which were as much for his own good as for his wife's. "I will never leave thee, nor forsake thee," Charles quoted from Hebrews 13:5. They both took comfort from the Twenty-third Psalm, especially David's reference to the Good Shepherd, "He restoreth my soul."

Charles was a young Presbyterian minister in Wellsville, New York. Members of his little congregation helped with the housework and cooking while Marcia was recovering.

Now, in 1865, just as the war ended, Marcia was about to deliver again. She was resting in bed at home when Charles, who was in his study at the church, heard from a visitor that President Lincoln, who had been shot the day before, had died. The visitor left the newspaper so Charles could read the full account.

Stunned, Charles wondered: *Shall I mention this shocking news to Marcia? Will the trauma of this news affect the birth of the baby?* Charles Livingston asked God for wisdom, and he prayed for the safety of his wife and child.

With his eyes still closed, Charles thought of President Lincoln and the many problems facing the nation and people in his community in the aftermath of the war so recently ended. He felt overwhelmed. *So many problems,* he thought. *A crisis at home, a whole church full of people needing help. Sermons to prepare. The sick to be visited. What is expected of me?*

He felt the pressures of life in full measure at that moment. He poured out his heart to God. Then, his burden somewhat lifted, he went back to work on his sermon.

The following day, Charles left his office at noon and headed home. He had left Marcia in the care of two ladies from the church, with instructions to send someone to call him "if anything happens."

When Charles arrived at the house his wife was already in labor, and in an hour and a half she had delivered a baby girl. Within minutes the baby had problems breathing. The midwife sent one of the ladies helping her to call the doctor.

News of the struggle for life of the baby girl soon reached many of the homes in the small village; concerned Christian people all over the hamlet were praying for the baby and for the Livingston family. It was a very emotional time for everyone, that April 16, 1865, in Wellsville. President Abraham Lincoln had died the day before. News of related events came over the "wire" to a grieving nation. The Livingston baby lived. That news came to neighbors and parishioners by word of mouth, and brought a measure of gladness into the midst of the sadness over the president's death.

Charles and Marcia had agreed that she would name the baby if it were a boy, and he would name the child if it were a girl. He named the new baby Grace.

Grace's mother had taken her place in the world as "Marcia Macdonald." The Macdonald family roots traced back to an old clan in Scotland. Some of the Macdonalds had come to America in the mid-1700s, settling in New England and New York.

For a young woman who had lost one baby and who had nearly lost the second child as well, Marcia was remarkably stable. She was steadfast in her faith in God, for she had been brought up in a home with firm Christian teaching.

Others in her family exhibited the same steadfast faith even in times of tragedy. One of her relatives was Horatio Spafford, a well-respected Chicago businessman. "Uncle Horatio" was a man of deep faith, interested in all subjects biblical. In his Bible reading he observed that Jesus would come back to this earth to rule as king. His understanding of this in biblical sequence was, perhaps, lacking. He apparently did not know that in God's time line certain things must precede Christ's physical return to earth as king, and that some of those events had not yet taken place. Nevertheless, in his zeal to be on hand, should this happen in his lifetime, and to further his biblical studies while he waited, he made plans to visit the Holy Land with his family. Horatio had to tidy up some business before he could depart, but his wife, who was a capable person in her own right, agreed to go ahead with their four girls and find a house in Jerusalem. Horatio would follow in a few week's time.

As Horatio made his final preparations to set sail, word came that the ship on which his family had been traveling had gone down at sea. His wife only was rescued; she sent her husband a cable with the message, "Saved alone." Horatio immediately set sail to rejoin her. The shock easily could have broken any man but, in his grief, Horatio met with his best Friend. He poured out his heart to God. As his ship neared the spot where his family went down, he wrote:

When peace, like a river, attendeth my way,
*   When sorrows like sea billows roll;*
Whatever my lot, Thou hast taught me to say,
*   It is well, it is well with my soul.*

Though Satan should buffet, though trials should
*   come,*

Let this blest assurance control,
That Christ has regarded my helpless estate,
And hath shed His own blood for my soul.

My sin—oh, the bliss of this glorious thought—
My sin—not in part, but the whole—
Is nailed to the cross and I bear it no more,
Praise the Lord, praise the Lord, O my soul!

And, Lord, haste the day when the faith shall be
sight,
The clouds be rolled back as a scroll,
The trump shall resound and the Lord shall descend,
"Even so"—it is well with my soul.

Here was a man of strong faith in God who knew how to live. He could wrestle with death and destruction and win. In his darkest hour, Horatio G. Spafford had put on paper a hymn that would comfort millions of people for generations to come. It was simply entitled: "It Is Well with My Soul."

Marcia Macdonald Livingston, steadfast in the faith that worked in those around her, passed that formula for joy and peace on to her daughter Grace.

The Livingston family, a well-known American clan, had established itself in America one hundred years before the Revolutionary War. Robert Livingston was perhaps the first of them. He left his home region of Roxburghshire, Scotland, and arrived in Massachusetts in 1673. Later he moved to Albany County, New York.

The Albany countryside had been settled some years before, mostly by the Wallons, a prominent Dutch clan. Other Livingstons arrived in New York, having obtained land grants from the king, since America was a Crown colony of Great Britain. The Scottish Livingstons, as well as other Scottish clans that had emigrated to New York, soon integrated with the Dutch immigrants and absorbed through bloodline and culture the staid technical and trade-oriented bent of the Dutch, mixed with the thrifty but humorous traits of the Scots. This blend of traits, mixed with the tenacious, fighting spirit and bravery that has kept the Scots and Dutch from being absorbed by their larger and stronger neighbors for hundreds of years, made for hardy pioneers on the edge of the North American frontier.

When America called her men to fight for freedom, and a new order of self-government was envisioned, the Livingstons were heavily involved. Col. James Livingston and Lt. Col. Richard Livingston formed the First Canadian Regiment which had a strength of about 450 officers and men. Along with other volunteer regiments, they patrolled the northern border of New York during the Revolutionary War. Livingstons in other regiments also volunteered for service.

The family was well entrenched in New York and some of its most distinguished kinsmen helped draft and sign the major documents that are the foundation of the United States' brand of democracy. Many Livingston sons and daughters were active in politics, law, religion, and education. They were a rare breed, often laboring to help others with no regard for their own safety or personal enrichment. With others like them, they became a minority that composed the backbone for the majority that were working toward a successful democracy. They were tolerant of, as well as interested in, others' viewpoints, and willing to learn. They were progressive survivors in a still new and untamed land. Charles came from a family that was, perhaps, as aristocratic as the New World would produce; aristocratic in the sense that they were the best representatives of the new age of democracy.

Both Charles and Marcia had been raised in that spirit of serving others. They met at a church conference and became attracted to each other. Their backgrounds were similar. After a year or so of courting, they were married at her home. Theirs was a love that endured.

HAPPINESS HILL

CHAPTER II

MARCIA MACDONALD loved to tell stories when she was a young child, and now as a mother she told bedtime stories to her daughter. The tales often ended with a moral, or were teaching tools; sometimes they were quite humorous.

Storytelling was a family art, but Marcia and her older sister, Belle, were dubbed by their father as "the two queens of bedtime tales." Both the girls began writing at an early age, and coauthored many of their early writings. After they were separated by schooling and marriage, they developed their own writing careers. However, Belle and Marcia often consulted each other about writing.

Since the two sisters sometimes worked as partners on their writings, Belle shared the use of her new typewriter, bought with what she earned from the sales of some of her magazine articles. It was one of the first all-capital Remingtons. Grace, even as a little girl, was shown how to use the machine, and was soon carefully spelling short words on bits of scrap paper.

Marcia developed a successful writing career, although not to the same extent as her sister. She authored several books, and a feature column in a Chicago-based weekly magazine, *The Interior.*

Marcia wrote quite a profusion of children's stories for Sunday school papers, and in 1883 she wrote her only full-length book for children, entitled, *The Story of Puff.* It was the story of a baby canary that was taken from its nest by a small girl. She kept the bird as a pet and named him Puff. Though at first he was sad, soon he became an important part of the family. But Puff had growing-up pains. He made some new friends who, regrettably, led him far astray. Puff was a prodigal canary, unhappy until he returned home again.

The last few paragraphs of the book give the flavor of Marcia's writing:

I am at last perfectly happy and contented. I have tried everything I thought I wanted, and it wasn't what I thought it was, and now I am back in the old place, and here was what I wanted all the time and I didn't know it. Silly Puff!

It is out of fashion to put a moral after a story, but I am going to have one to mine.

MORAL: If you should be thrown into bad company, don't take their advice.
It takes only a little minute to do something that may cause months of sorrow.
Be content.

The little book had 105 pages and 27 illustrations. The cover featured a colored picture of an open-sided wheelbarrow full of flowers, and a canary flying over it. The text and the illustrations had a softer tone than many of today's children's books with their psychedelic colors.

The best work the sisters did together was a collaboration entitled *By Way of the Wilderness*. It was a romance novel and, in many ways the later works of Grace Livingston Hill reflect its influence. The sisters did not continue in this line of writing, however.

The Livingstons were a family of communicators, and Charles was not only thought of as an outstanding speaker but as an interesting writer as well. He frequently contributed to religious newspapers and magazines. His subjects were theological rather than fiction, but they were entertaining, as well as informative.

Marcia's sister Isabella attended Oneida Seminary, where her brother-in-law was a professor. While she was a student there, she was courted by Gustavus Rossenberg Alden, a young student at Auburn Theological Seminary. Ross (if anyone ever needed a nickname he did) and Isabella fell in love. In May 1866, they were married by Charles Livingston in a wedding ceremony at the Macdonald home, where many relatives and friends had gathered. The wedding seemed more than just a joining of the bride and groom; a bond was formed that day between the two families that lasted many years.

Isabella was twenty-five years old when she was married. Grace watched the beauty and excitement of the wedding from the arms of her maiden Aunt Jewel. Grace was observant and lively for a thirteen-month only child. It seemed unlikely that an aunt and niece, with an age difference of twenty-four years, should one day be such good friends. "Auntie Belle" became Grace's ideal. Her mother and aunt served as role models of what a woman should be before her God, her family, and her community.

Grace's early life was devoid of luxuries. Her father was very well respected, but as a pastor he received a very low salary. The people of the church, however, were extremely kind and shared with their pastor as best they could. When needs became obvious, people were ready and willing to help.

The ladies of the church were always alert to birthdays and anniversaries. It was touching when, on the Livingstons' sixth wedding anniversary, two ladies arrived at the Livingston home with packages, said, "Happy Anniversary," and left. Each neatly wrapped parcel contained a lovely pound cake. Somehow or other, almost every lady in the church decided a pound cake would be the perfect gift and delivered her tribute to the church office or to the Livingston home. Within two days the family had collected fourteen pound cakes! They decided that they could not possibly give any of these offerings of love away in such a small community without hurting someone's feelings. So, under cover of darkness, Charles buried eleven pound cakes in the backyard!

The home atmosphere was loving. Relatives often visited and among them, of course, were Marcia's sister Isabella, and her husband Ross. Isabella was full of fun and surprises. She always took a keen interest in listening to little Grace tell her original stories.

In 1877, on Grace's twelfth birthday, Isabella (Auntie Belle) gave her a very special gift. She had listened carefully some months before while Grace told a story of two warmhearted children. As she listened, Auntie Belle typed it out on her marvelous typewriter. Now she gave Grace a bound copy of that story. It was a little hardback book, complete with woodcut illustrations. What a surprise! The printing and binding had been done by D. Lothrop Company, in Boston, publishers of most of Isabella's *Pansy* books.

"Now, Grace," said Auntie Belle, "I have some important advice to give you. This is your first book, and I am your first publisher. But in the future you must write your stories down and find a publisher on your own. Your mother and I will help you, but you must discipline yourself early in life to your writing."

How true those words proved to be! Mother and aunt did help in the years ahead, but the discipline of writing was literally forced upon Grace later in her life.

As a young girl, Grace could read aloud very well, and with expression. Her father suffered from eyestrain caused by his constant study, and in the evenings when the gaslight made his eyes ache, he would often call his daughter to read the newspaper to him. He was interested in politics and current events and often made comments and predictions about trends. This stimulated conversation, and in the following weeks or months Grace found her father's perceptions were often correct.

Grace was a strong-willed person, as were the other ladies in the family. Sometimes this led to what appeared as conflict. She would not avoid an argument and carried on disputes with her mother for years. They were deeply devoted to each other and very loyal, but they loved to argue. "Discuss," they would have called it! In a way, it "was all in good fun." They never meant to hurt each other and the debates got loud only occasionally; but the pot was always bubbling. In later years, other members of her own family joined in the "fun," but some suffered from the constant "bickering." Mealtimes were particularly good arenas for petty quarrels. One member of the family says she still gets indigestion thinking about it.

Luxuries were few in the Livingston household, but the love of beauty was strong in Grace, and she dreamed of lovely things. Once she saw a very stylish lady with a really stunning feather fan. Grace knew she could never afford a fan like that one, but she took special note of how the fan was constructed. When her father killed two of their chickens, she saved the feathers to construct her fan. For a few cents she bought the items needed and made the fan she wanted.

She often went to great effort to produce what she wanted. She was not at all resentful of the lack of money, for she enjoyed the ingenuity of making something fine from very little.

Charles was a keenly sought-after preacher and lecturer. He was often invited to speak at meetings away from his home church. He worked well with his elder boards at the various churches he served, and they were willing to share their pastor with other churches. Grace often traveled with her father by horse and buggy to small outlying churches. Their conversation was lively and varied.

Sometimes father and daughter traveled by train; sitting side by side, they enjoyed discussing all sorts of subjects. If there were small children seated nearby, young Grace entertained them with wonderful stories. Grace was more than a companion to her father or an amusement to strangers on these trips. She always helped with the Sunday school wherever they went. She had gained a good knowledge of the Bible from her parents and could make its truths come alive to the small children with whom she worked. Grace traveled and helped her father in this way into her early twenties.

The times she enjoyed most were the evenings when the family gathered and read aloud to each other. These were the times she missed most when she went away to school. First she went to Elmira College, but after one term she was so homesick that she was allowed to come home. She had done well in high school, and she wanted a good education, but could not face being away from her parents. After some soul-searching, she tried going to school again, this time to Cincinnati Art School. She was so aware of beauty that she wanted to study art. She had done chalk drawings before large groups when she had accompanied her father on his speaking trips, and had also produced several paintings which her family and friends felt showed promise. She progressed well at school, but before long she was overcome with homesickness again. Thoughts of art as a career ended, but painting became a hobby she enjoyed all her life.

Grace felt like a failure, dropping out of school and coming home to explain, "I was too homesick to stay." It seemed so silly. She was struggling in late adolescence to find herself, to set a course for her life. She was no longer a girl, and yet not quite a woman. Life seemed bleak and prayers seemed unanswered. But years later she realized that she had just been growing up.

OUT OF THE STORM

CHAPTER III

CHARLES LIVINGSTON'S health was failing. He had special difficulty with his throat, and almost continual bronchitis. The presbytery sent him on a convalescent leave to Florida for one month to see if his health would improve.

It was a new adventure for Grace and gave her, at least for a short time, a chance to forget her problems, busy as she was with helping her mother pack and plan for the month they would be away.

The age of steam was at its height, still causing excitement, and the family traveled by rail. The massive engines struck a romantic chord, even as they do today, when we relive their glory on film or in books. And the trip! It was thrilling to see new places and meet new people. It was relaxing to read and talk without interruption. It was grand to be called to dinner and be served a full-course meal at a table in the dining car, and watch the countryside go gliding by. Then at last to arrive in Florida, to feel the warm sunshine, and see oranges on the trees. It was quite a contrast to the gray, overcast skies and barren trees of New York.

What fun it was to be outdoors in the dead of winter and enjoy the spring-like weather. Grace's eye for beauty added to her enjoyment. The lush semitropical foliage was a delight to her. Oranges were ripening on the trees, and hibiscus and bougainvillea and other tropical plants were in full flower. Best of all, her father felt better. The rest and the milder climate seemed to be what he needed.

Charles requested a transfer, and within a few months the family had moved to Winter Park, Florida, near Orlando, where he was assigned a church. It was the summer of 1886, and Grace was twenty-one. The move was exciting, but it was the first summer in several years that the family could not spend their vacation at Chautauqua Lake in New York.

Daily routine in Winter Park was very much as it had been in New York. Grace's father carried on his work with his church and spoke at meetings. Both father and mother continued writing articles for magazines and papers. Some of their relatives came to visit.

The Florida summer was extremely hot, humid, and "crawling with bugs"—not at all what the family was used to. Charles wrote to his family back East: "Wearing a coat and tie to preach in, on a July Sunday in Florida, is pure madness." But it was expected of him, so he did it. His throat felt much better and his health was so improved that putting up with the disadvantages of the heat were well worth the effect it had on his body.

The whole family missed the summer meetings at Chautauqua, where they had enjoyed the company of friends and relatives. As an alternative, the family attended the Mt. Dora Conferences near where they lived. These meetings were somewhat like the Bible conferences or retreats that are popular nowadays. Each week a nationally known speaker was featured. The conferences were greatly enjoyed, but they lacked the variety of the Chautauqua meetings which covered more than biblical topics.

Living in Winter Park in the late 1800s was primitive compared to life in Wellsville, New York. Sidewalks were made of board slats. Small lizards, often seen lying on the bushes, turned light green or dark brown to blend in with the twig on which they rested. Sometimes the harmless little creatures got into the house. They hid behind curtains and roller shades, and stalked tiny insects for lunch. Enormous spiders, with leg spans of up to five inches, lived in the dark of the closets. From time to time they would emerge and run across the ceiling after their prey, or bound two body lengths at a leap, chasing a palmetto bug across the floor. The women, especially, detested the spiders, and wondered how to get rid of them for good.

"Oh, no!" said a neighbor, in the local drawl. "You nevah kill a house spider! Why Honny, you'll nevah have a moth in yo' closet if just one house spider makes his home there. They're as good as owning a cedar chest and don't cost you a penny." Such wonders and revelations were cause for humorous letters to friends back home. What the neighbor said was true. It was another world.

The move to Florida had not eliminated the problems Grace had faced back in New York. She needed some kind of work to occupy her time, but jobs were not easy to find in Winter Park. However, the church needed a secretary. It was a part-time job without pay; still, Grace volunteered and worked with her father at the church three days a week. Other days she worked with her mother at home or visited needy families in the town and surrounding countryside, helping however she could.

Grace and her mother were eager to make plans for the family to attend Chautauqua again. They wanted to make reservations for their favorite guest house in plenty of time for the coming summer. Charles, in his kind way, brought them back to reality. "If you look at our bank account and what we can save between now and then, and if you add up the expenses of traveling from here to New York and back, and the costs of Chautauqua, you will find that it is impossible to make the trip this coming summer."

Grace and her mother weren't convinced, and they

spent several days discussing and figuring every aspect of costs and income. By the time they had exhausted all possibilities they reluctantly agreed that Charles had figured right. But Grace did not give up. She wanted so badly to go, she was almost in tears. "I'll write a book," she said. "If I write a book and sell it, can we all go?"

"I've been telling you to develop your writing," reminded her mother.

"If you earn the money to take us all to Chautauqua, Grace, your mother and I will be happy to go with you," said her father with a speculative smile.

Within a week Grace was well into her story. "I'll show you the manuscript when I've finished the first draft," she told her mother. "Then I'll ask you for some editorial help."

"She's at it with a vengeance," remarked Marcia, as she looked up from her knitting as she and Charles sat by the fire one chilly evening.

Charles watched his daughter at the desk and spoke to her loudly enough to break her chain of thought. "Grace, stop your writing for a few minutes and come and read to me, dear."

"Let me finish this page and I'll be right there," she replied.

Charles realized something that night about his daughter, that perhaps his wife had already grasped. Grace was going to be a writer. She had the grit to follow through. She was rising to a need in her life. She could be interrupted without getting upset because she had her story under control. *I'm not going to worry about this girl getting married or finding meaningful work anymore,* he thought. *She's found what she likes to do most.*

Soon Grace was beside him, reading the newspaper aloud. The Livingstons were at peace with themselves that nippy night in November 1886.

Years later Grace wrote about the memorable times in Winter Park:

And the evenings! Oh, the evenings! The crown of the days! The time to which we all looked forward as to a goal, when our work was done! Those evenings are bright spots in my youth. Especially the evenings of the years we all spent together in Florida, when the sun went down sharply and the light went velvet black suddenly, till the great tropical moon came out. Those long evenings when the soft, dense darkness shut us into a cheerful supper table, father and mother, aunts and cousins.

After we had hustled through the dishes we all gathered in the big sitting room around the open fire for family worship. Yes, we were as old-fashioned as that! We had family worship both morning and evening. And I am not of those modern ones who mention such things to scoff at them, and say how sick we became of religion because of them, and to blame on that any present indifference to God and the

Bible. I look to those times as the most precious, the most beautiful, the most powerful influence that came into my life. I thank God for a family that worshiped Him morning and evening, and gave me a knowledge of, and a love for, the Bible and the things of the Kingdom of Heaven. In the morning either my father or my uncle would read the Scripture. There would be a hymn in which we all joined, and then prayer. In the evening we would all recite verses in turn before the prayer. I can hear their voices now— Grandmother's voice too, quavering out old hymns, while she stayed with us before she went home to Heaven.

*"Lord in the morning Thou shalt hear
My voice ascending high . . ."*

"Abide with me, fast falls the even tide . . ."

I listened as my family talked with God and I became inevitably acquainted with the Lord Jesus, so that I never could be troubled by the doubts of today. I think the secret of this is that my fathers lived the faith they preached. I saw that it worked, for I saw Jesus Christ in their daily lives.

By Christmas Grace's book was completed. It had been rewritten several times and was now in final form, handwritten in a lined exercise book. Grace borrowed a typewriter, and she and her mother took turns typing and doing the housework until the job was done.

The book was entitled *A Chautauqua Idyl.* She had written about the very place where she wanted to go! The manuscript was sent to D. Lothrop Company. This was the publisher who had put together *The Essel-stynes*, that little book that Auntie Belle had surprised Grace with on her twelfth birthday.

Grace and the family waited and wondered whether the *Idyl* would be accepted or rejected. Fortunately, with Christmas so near, there were lots of activities at home and at the church to keep them all busy.

In mid-January, the waiting was over. Grace received a letter from Lothrop. The book was accepted and a contract was enclosed. The publisher was very complimentary of her work. A copy of her manuscript had been sent to Bishop Vincent, who had started the Chautauqua movement, and he had given the book a favorable review! Another copy of the manuscript had gone to Edward Everett Hale, Chaplain of the United States Senate, with a request for his review. "We plan to use Mr. Hale's letter as an introduction to your book," the publisher wrote. He enclosed a copy of Mr. Hale's letter:

I have read Miss Livingston's little idyl with much pleasure. I cannot but think that if the older and more sedate members of the Chautauqua circles will read it, they will find that there are grains of profit in it; hidden grains, perhaps, but none the worse for being hidden at the first, if they only discover them.

*Miss Livingston has herself evidently understood the
spirit of the movement in which the Chautauqua
reading circles are engaged. That is more than can
be said for everyone who expresses an opinion upon
them. It is because she expresses no opinion, but
rather tells, very simply, the story of the working out
of the plan, that I am glad you are going to publish
her little poem: for a poem it is, excepting that it is
not in verse or in rhyme. Believe me,*

> *Very truly yours,*
> *Edward Everett Hale*

Grace shared the thrill of the acceptance of her book
with her mother, then they both hurried to the church
to share the good news with Charles. In the excitement
of being published, Grace hadn't thought of payment
for the work. Now seated with her father and mother in
the church office, she reread the letters and, for the first
time, examined the contract. Grace read it aloud, and
her father agreed that she had earned enough money
for them all to visit Chautauqua that coming summer.
Grace signed the contract and mailed it back to the
publisher the same day.

That night during family prayers, they all thanked
God for His special gift to them that day.

A Chautauqua Idyl was published in the spring of
1887 so that it would be ready for sale during the conference that summer. It was a simple allegory about
flowers and birds and a clear running brook that started

a Chautauqua of their own. One of the flowers had seen the meetings for people and introduced the idea one day when some other flowers and birds voiced a need for more fellowship.

"Let's have a Chautauqua!" cried the brook.
"But how can we," said the wise-eyed violet,
"when we know so little about it?"
"I will tell you all I know," said Bachelor [bachelor button flower—Ed.] graciously.

After much planning the whole concept was put together, and the birds and the flowers and the brook had a wonderful conference. Grace Livingston recorded the plans in her book:

And then all the lily-bells will chime out and call to prayer, the great red sun will come up and lead, and our little Chautauqua will open.
You will hear the sweet notes of praise from the bird choir, and prayers will rise from the flowers like sweet incense; you will see and hear it all, but will you remember that it is all to show forth the glory of God?

The book had twenty-two pen-and-ink illustrations, the binding was blue hardback, and it sold for sixty cents.

Bishop Vincent, the founder of the New York Chautauqua, always spoke to the large assembly at "old first night." There, before a gathering of several thousand people, he announced the publication of the book and praised *A Chautauqua Idyl,* by Miss Grace Livingston. It was the first public recognition of hundreds that would follow in the coming years.

Grace had no sooner returned home from what she said was the "most exciting holiday of my life," than she started another book. The idea came as she was perusing one of the devotional books that was on display at the bookstore on the Chautauqua grounds.

Her plan was simple. The best-selling author on the subject of Chautauqua was her Auntie Belle, who sometimes wrote under the name Pansy. She had written *Four Girls at Chautauqua, Chautauqua Girls at Home,* and many other books that interested the ladies who were in Chautauqua "circles" (reading and art clubs at the local level). Grace had decided to take quotes from her aunt's books and couple them with quotes from the Bible, one for each day of the year.

By mid-1888 the book was complete, and was published later that year by D. Lothrop Company. Her aunt wrote the preface.

I have followed with absorbing interest the compilation of this volume. As I have watched the fair young head bent from day to day over "The Deathless

Book," making quotations from its inspired pages that should repeat and emphasize my own thoughts, there has been a grateful, uplifting, humbling realization of the fact that I was being linked with immortality! For certainly the words that accompany my simple ones make each page glow with a light that shall have power to shine even to the very gates of the eternal city.

Moreover, as I watched the thoughtful face of the compiler brighten and flush, and her eyes grow earnest while her heart took in some solemn charge of the Master, I have felt that, as she transmitted it to paper, there went with it a prayer that the Holy Spirit who had guided her choice, would use these pages in a way to lead some souls daily higher, and higher, even into the "shining light" of the "perfect day."

In this wish and prayer I join her earnestly, as the little book goes out to do its work.

Pansy

The book was titled, *Pansies for Thoughts*. It was a small pocket-size hardback, about six inches by four inches by three-quarters of an inch thick. It was bound in blue cloth, with the title stamped in gold on the front and spine, and gold outlines of pansies scattered over the cover. The page edges were covered in polished gold leaf.

Inside there were daily devotional thoughts for a

whole year, each taken from a Pansy book, with the title
of the book given. And each devotional thought was followed by an appropriate Bible quotation. Following are
two examples:

*Of course some changes must come; nothing ever
stayed for any length of time just as it was; but what
would the change be? It came in an unexpected
manner; perhaps that is the common way with
change.*
Judge Burnham's Daughter

*Watch ye, therefore: for ye know not when the
master of the house cometh . . . Lest coming suddenly
he find you sleeping. (Mark 13:35, 36)*

*I don't know the end of any story that is being
lived—not yours or mine, for instance; but the Lord
does; and I would much rather have Him do all the
planning.*
An Endless Chain

*But he knoweth the way that I take: when he hath
tried me, I shall come forth as gold. (Job 23:10)*

*His wisdom ever waketh,
His sight is never dim;
He knows the way He taketh,
And I will walk with Him.*

It was the next step in a young career, but Grace was a storyteller. This was the first of only two nonfiction books she would ever write; the next would not be written until 1919 when she wrote, with Evangeline Booth, a history of the Salvation Army during World War I. But that would be thirty-one years and twenty-eight books later!

Grace was by now thinking of writing as a career, but she would take another turn or two in her search for a life's work before she settled down to writing in earnest. She was still young and loved people and sports and it seemed that writing might be just a little too "slow" for her, at least for now.

SUNRISE

CHAPTER IV

INTER PARK was not an old town. In fact it was very new. The first log cabin was built in the area in 1858, about three miles from the Osceola Station of the South Florida Railroad.

In the late 1870s, six hundred acres were purchased to form a planned community. The original settlers were from the Northeast, mostly from Massachusetts and New York; they built their homes and planned an entire town on the plot. The streets these early settlers planned are still named after them: Chapman, Chase, Comstock, Lyman, Fairbanks, Webster, Pulsifer.

These men conceived a lofty plan:

. . . they set out searching among their numerous acquaintances by expensive and alluring advertising

among others, for the kind of settlers who would fit into their scheme, men and women of intelligence, culture, character, taste and means. (History of Orange County Florida, *by William Fremont Blackman)*

Here they proposed to create a first class resort for Northern and Southern men of wealth, where amidst orange groves and beautiful lakes, and surrounded by all the conveniences and luxuries that energy, enterprise, and wealth can devise and command, a community of grand winter homes, a resort second to none in the South. . . . (Sanford South Florida Journal, *Sept. 8, 1881)*

Among the earliest members to join the original group were Rev. Gustavus Rossenberg Alden and his wife, Isabella (Grace's Aunt Belle and author "Pansy"). The new community sounded interesting to them and they also hoped the climate would be beneficial to their son. Several years later, the Reverend Mr. Alden wrote in a letter to a friend: "My son went to Florida as an invalid, by the advice of his physician; he left with health fully restored."

It was the Aldens who persuaded the Livingstons to visit Florida for the sake of Charles's health, and by 1886 the two sisters were living in the same town and working together again on their writings.

The Aldens were very much a part of the small town's

activities. The greatest undertaking, by far, was the proposed founding of a college. The idea had started with Lucy A. Cross, the headmistress of a private girls' school in Daytona Beach. She approached the newly formed Florida Congregational Association with her idea, and read a paper during its first annual meeting held at Winter Park back in 1884. Frederick W. Lyman had been talking about a college for Winter Park since 1882, so Miss Cross's paper strengthened his conviction. Dr. Edward P. Hooker, pastor of the Congregational Church of Winter Park, preached a moving sermon advocating Christian education, which lent awareness and support to the cause through his parishioners.

At the second annual meeting of the Congregational Association of Florida in 1885, it was agreed that the Association should start a college as part of its "mission." Site selection for the campus was done by initiating a very straightforward procedure. The location of the proposed school was to be put out to bid. Several towns considered suitable were contacted and the six towns made proposals:

Mt. Dora bid land for a campus, real estate, lumber, pledges, and a microscope, all with a total value of $35,564.

Daytona offered $11,500 cash, and a site on the Atlantic Ocean which they valued at $20,000.

Jacksonville offered a selection of sites plus cash of $13,000.

Interlachen offered $12,000 in cash and pledges.

Orange City offered $9,326 cash, work at a value of $559, lumber valued at $150, and land at $1,800, for a total of $11,835.

Winter Park bid cash, stock, and land valued at $114,180.

The delegates from the Association chose Winter Park, and later suggested that the school be named Rollins College because of the gift of $50,000 "in real estate given by Mr. Rollins, a Christian gentleman. . . ." In fact, Mr. Rollins had been considering helping to start a Christian college in the Midwest, and had set aside part of his estate for the purpose of Christian education. God had placed him at the right place at the right time to fulfill his pledge.

The Association lost no time in beginning construction of the college buildings and recruiting a staff of instructors. Dr. E. P. Hooker was named school president.

Work will begin this summer on the building for the recitation rooms and cottages for dormitories. Dr. Hooker and others will go at once to the North to raise further endowment and make arrangements to open the College term. . . . The best teachers that can be found will be secured. . . . (Sanford South Florida Journal, *April 29, 1885)*

The school opened on November 4, 1885. Tuition was $18 per term; board, $48 (later reduced to $36); furnished room with light, $12. Total costs for the year (three terms) was $234. There were fifty-three charter students enrolled on the opening day.

Although Rollins was started as a college, it also ran a preparatory department, and Raymond Alden, Grace's cousin, finished his high school training there. He was one of the charter students, and in the following year his father became a trustee of the school.

Raymond was a popular figure on the campus. Many of the girls had read the *Pansy* books written by his mother and, because of Raymond's good looks, he soon picked up the nickname of "Lord Pansy." But Raymond also distinguished himself as a scholar, and was admired greatly for his own aptitude as a writer, even in his teen years.

During these years the Livingstons and the Aldens enjoyed many evenings together. They worked on books together, traveled back to New York together, and always enjoyed each other's company.

Within a short time the college had become the pride of the town, and by the 1887–88 term had grown to 164 students. But during the following year a yellow fever epidemic swept central Florida and many students became seriously ill. The epidemic started in the summer and a number of students who had gone north for the summer did not return that fall. The enrollment plummeted to 85 students.

Almost everyone in the town was in some way involved with the college. It brought cultural activity to Winter Park as well as an influx of educated and interesting people. One such person was Frederick Starr, Ph.D., who joined the faculty in 1887 when science was added to the curriculum. His main subject was anthropology, which was a relatively new area of science at the time for many colleges and universities.

Dr. Starr, well-traveled and brilliant, soon struck up a friendship with Raymond. He was invited to the Alden home and enjoyed the fellowship of both the Aldens and the Livingstons. Almost at once, Dr. Starr was attracted to Grace Livingston. He admired her interest in beauty and her enthusiasm for life; she admired his intelligence and was fascinated by the stories of his interesting adventures. He was charming, yet he was sometimes abrasive, and occasionally offensive to his seniors with his dogmatic positions on many subjects, especially world affairs. However, everyone agreed that Dr. Starr was well informed and had a fine mind. The relationship grew between Frederick and Grace, and they were often seen together at social functions in the town or on campus.

To Grace, everything seemed young and new and joyful. The town was new, the school was new, and romance was new. She had almost found herself, and her new career as a writer had begun to develop. These were the years when she wrote *A Chautauqua Idyl* (1887), and *Pansies for Thoughts* (1888).

In January of 1889, Grace started work on her next book, a short novel. The work was progressing nicely but she was dedicating only about one hour a day to writing. Writing was still a hobby; there was no pressure or need to write now as there had been with the *Idyl.* Her needs were met, and she was busy working with her father at the church and her mother at home.

Early the same year, a rail line was initiated between Orlando and Winter Park, which helped the enrollment of the college and the growth of the town.

Transportation facilities for day students were immeasurably facilitated in February, 1889, when a five-mile narrow gauge scenic railroad, winding about the lakes from Orlando to Winter Park where it half circled the campus along Lake Virginia, was put into operation. Its cars were painted bright orange; its small wood-burner engine consumed pitch pine. Students have long since somewhat derisively but affectionately styled it "The Dinkey Line." So slow was its pace, claimed one wit, that after leaving Orlando he jumped off, walked a mile, sat down, prepared his assignment in Greek, and took a nap until awakened by the train catching up with him, where upon he rode the remainder of the distance to the campus. (The First Seven Years of Rollins College, *Rollins College Archives)*

One evening in May, Dr. Hooker, the President of Rollins College, dropped by for a visit at the Livingston home. He was just in time for the evening prayer and Bible reading. It was quite a gathering, he noted, with the Aldens also present. Three ladies, all of them authors, and, counting himself, three churchmen. He noted with a smile that Raymond could be anything he liked, since he was the top student in the academy program.

Charles chose a Scripture passage and they all took turns reading. As on every evening since Grace could remember, the family read together, talked, and then the evening ended in prayer. Dr. Hooker was happy to fellowship with them. It was an important time for every member of the family. Marcia was active in helping needy people in the community and mentioned prayer requests for the sick and needy. Charles asked for prayer for personal problems of people with whom he was counseling. If the problems were private ones, he did not mention the people by name, even to his family. He held his parishioners' confidence as a sacred trust. Grace mentioned friends and relatives for whom they should pray. Together as always, they thanked God for His goodness to them and for the provision of their own needs. Dr. Hooker requested prayer for the school and for additional staff.

After reading the Scriptures and a time of prayer, Dr. Hooker asked Grace if she would like to volunteer her services as Physical Education Director. Would she pray about it with the family and let him know her decision within a week? If she chose to help, the board would need to interview her.

Grace decided that she should help her parents at least part-time and offer her services to the college in the afternoons. So the interview was set.

Grace set off for the board interview with many misgivings. Freshman students were eighteen or nineteen years old and she was only twenty-four. That meant that senior students would be close to her age. Maybe she should request only freshman students. Strangely, the college where she had gone as a guest to play tennis did not seem such a friendly place that morning as she ascended the wide steps to the porch of the Administration Building.

After speaking to the receptionist, and after a short uneasy wait for the interview, Grace found herself comfortably seated in Dr. Hooker's office. He introduced her to the board members: Mr. Comstock, Mr. Fairbanks, Mr. Lyman and Mr. Rollins. The interview went well and Grace was accepted officially as Leader in Calisthenics and Heavy Gymnastics.

Grace enjoyed people and sports, and so the program

she started was a pleasure to both the teacher and the students and even to the people who came to watch!

Letters of appreciation for Grace's work came from both parents and students:

The Lyman Gymnasium at Rollins College is a great attraction to residents and visitors. The system of calisthenics and gymnastics, taught by Miss Livingston . . . is very pretty, and from five each afternoon the guest galleries are thronged with a delighted audience.

The letter referred to an exercise known as "wand drill," which was done with a polished stick, and was often executed by the entire class in slow motion. Fencing moves were performed plus an exercise routine. This class was as popular with the students as it was with the on-lookers.

. . . Grace Livingston, as we know her. She was one to know and never forget. She gathered the young men and boys together and helped them to settle some of the questions that every young man settles one way or another during his life—such as Sabbath observance—tobacco among men. (Dr. James S. Hawley, Plant City, Florida, Rollins College Archives)

Grace kept several notebooks filled with a variety of poems, thoughts and pledges. When her students were concerned about issues in their lives and really seemed to want to make some sort of commitment to God, Grace asked them to sign a pledge.

For example, a Rollins student signed this pledge:

Trusting the Lord Jesus Christ for strength, I promise Him that I will strive to do whatever He would like to have me do; that I will pray to Him, and read the Bible every day; and that just so far as I know how throughout my whole life, I will endeavour to lead a Christian life.

It was a pledge that everyone in the Christian Endeavor Society signed on becoming a member.

Grace continued to enjoy her work with the young people at the college; but, as in all jobs, situations developed that required dialogue with the administration. Grace wanted a uniform dress for her physical education classes, but that caused an amusing situation. Many years later, when Rollins College had its Fiftieth Anniversary Celebration, Grace was asked to speak. She was not able to attend, but wrote the following letter:

February 11th, 1935

My dear Mr. Hanna:

I certainly appreciate your kindness in sending me the copy of the appreciation for my humble work

*which you found in the Rollins records of long ago.
It brought tears to my eyes to read it. Though
perhaps I knew about it long ago—I did of course—
but I had forgotten it. The work certainly was a
work of love, and was most delightful and absorbing,
and gave me dear friends whose friendships have
lasted through the years. Just this fall I had the
pleasure while in Chicago of spending a little time in
company with Walter Flentye and his charming
family, and seeing again his lovely home where I
have visited before. I have letters from Katharine
Lyman often, and from Robert Benedict and his wife
Minnie Forest Benedict, and from Ruth Ford Atkin-
son, and others of the long ago; and my days spent
in Winter Park with the dear Rollins students will
ever stand out as a sweet and delightful experience.*

*The little incident of which I told you is exceed-
ingly amusing in the light of present day freedom
and daring in the matter of dress—or rather, undress.*

*Our new gymnasium was finished, the gift of Mr.
Frederick Lyman, and fitted out with apparatus, each
piece personally donated by some dear friend of the
college (I remember there was a handsome scale
donated by Mr. Fairbanks) and we were getting
ready for real work. Consequently I began a movement for uniform dress for classes. The uniform I
suggested for the girls was the same that had been
used in my classes when I was studying under Dr.*

William Anderson of Yale. It consisted of dark blue
serge suits, the blouses made high neck with sailor
collar and long sleeves, and a blue serge "divided
skirt" we called it then I think, though it was nothing
more than the simple bloomer skirt, made very full
with pleats so that the division was not at all visible
except in action. The legs were gathered over rubber
bands at the knee and fell over far enough to look
like a skirt coming a trifle below the knee. They were
very neat and graceful, worn with long black stock-
ings and gymnasium "sneakers," and though the
modern athlete may think otherwise, the outfit gave
entire freedom of action both in heavy and light gymnasium work.

With this outfit we had a plain tailored dark blue
serge skirt to wear in the street, which provided
against the necessity of much changing of costume
between classes.

I was to appear formally before the Faculty to talk
over the matter of costume for the gymnasium work,
and it never occurred to me it was going to be a difficult task to get what I had requested. I had personally been brought up in a most conservative
manner as to attire, and I was heartily in accord
with my father and mother on the subject. Decollete
in those days was much objected to by all good
Christian people. Even the little pointed V neck of all
our garments today was felt to be a little daring, for

most refined women wore high-necked dresses at
least in daytime, and many Christian people objected
to the evening clothes of the days.

So I was much amazed to find that all but two or
three of the Faculty were very doubtful about a thing
called a bloomer or a divided skirt, and failed to give
way at my eager description of its modesty and ap-
propriateness. Indeed some of them even felt they
were conceding a good deal to be willing for the girls
to wear such costume in classes by themselves,
separate from the boys—up to that time the boys and
girls had been together in their floor work of course.
But I was thoroughly outraged. Couldn't they see
what a stigma they would be putting upon me if the
girls and boys had to be separated when they wore
that garb? I waxed eloquent about the matter and
told how it was the only sensible garment, and more
modest than ordinary dress, and I said, "Why, I have
it on now and I can show it to you. I'll step into the
hall and take off this skirt and come back and let
you see how it looks."

One of the lady teachers tried to protest at this
daring offer, but I whisked into the hall before they
could stop me and walked back in my gymnasium
dress, and in reality it was a pretty graceful affair.
Even now it might be thought so. There was nothing
ugly nor clumsy about it, and in truth it was not
quite as short as all stylish ladies wore in the street

and in the evening and everywhere, just a few short seasons ago.

But the effect on the troubled Faculty was astounding.

They sat in a circle with downcast eyes, hands in their laps, feeling perhaps that a great crisis in the college affairs was upon them. Only the two brave ladies who had been privileged to see the skirt before and were in hearty accord with me about it looked up with serene countenances and smiled upon me. The others remained with downcast eyes, and slowly, one by one, cast furtive sideways glances first at my toes, and then cautiously letting their frightened eyes travel upward till they got the whole effect, they one by one drew sighs of relief and permitted their eyes to resume a normal outlook on the world once again.

But it was dear old Dr. Hooker, the beloved president, who broke the silence first, with a voice that fairly lilted with relief.

"I think," said he, smiling around upon his teachers and professors, "that this dress is much more modest than the garb that is worn in social life. I can see nothing whatever objectionable in it. In fact I heartily approve it."

There was never any more said about it. But the dim memory of the caution and care of those other days that were so dear lights up pleasantly in con-

trast with these days when care and caution are scattered to the breeze, and there seem to be so few restraints in the world where we are feeling our way into new things. One wonders if they will find in the new ways things better than the old?

This has been written very hastily, and was a mere incident anyway, in a life that was full of joys and thrills and sorrows too, yet beloved to look back upon.

I hope you will pardon my delay and forgive a busy person who is not as indifferent as she may seem to be.

With all best wishes,

Very sincerely,

Grace Livingston Hill

WHERE TWO WAYS MET

C H A P T E R V

SUMMER'S shimmering heat came early to Winter Park in 1890. Dawn blazed clear each day and by early afternoon even the most devoted warm weather fancier was seeking shade and a cool drink. Thankfully, some relief came almost every afternoon in the form of massive thunderstorms that lasted only a few minutes. This seemed to clear the air and cool off the evenings. But the summer promised to be long and hot. The best solution to the problem was to get on the train and go north!

When the school year finished, the Livingstons, Aldens, and many other families journeyed up the eastern seaboard to visit relatives in the cooler Northeast. A number of them met again at Chautauqua later in the summer.

Chautauqua has been designated by Henry James as the "middle-class heaven." It was then less than middle class and perhaps less than heaven, if one may reckon that state of bliss by the degree of physical comfort. One slept upon "relief maps," as the artist Frank Beard described the lumpy mattresses. One ate awful things upon picnic tables with tin forks and shared spoons. But across the picnic table Dr. Frederick Starr laughed with you at the simple fare and talked about Neolithic man. . . .

Stimulus to mind, imagination, and thought—of course, it was. And it furnished the particular stimulus which started Grace Livingston upon her career.

Dr. Frederick Starr, so interesting, so charming, so popular, so dogmatic! It was an honor for Grace to be with him. There were so many single girls at the conference grounds and yet Frederick seemed to enjoy her company most. They played tennis and attended lectures together. To Grace it was a friendship, but she could feel that it was getting to be more than that to Frederick Starr. She suggested they not spend so much time together until they returned to Florida. This would give them a chance to mix more with old friends and make new ones. He agreed.

Grace's newest book, *A Little Servant*, had been published just in time for the opening week of Chautauqua, and it was announced at the conference. Many people came up to congratulate her on her latest achievement. One of her admirers, Rev. Thomas Franklin Hill, asked to accompany her to the vesper service that evening. Everyone called him Frank.

Frank Hill proved every bit as intelligent as Frederick Starr, but with completely different interests and without the flair or eccentric habits of the professor. The Hills were from a family of preachers. Rev. John Hill, Frank's father, was a Presbyterian minister with a church in Shelbyville, Tennessee, and Frank had a church near Pittsburgh, Pennsylvania.

Educated at Princeton University, Frank was given a scholarship to do graduate work at Edinburgh University in Scotland. His background was much like Grace's, with a family of strong Christians eager to share the gospel and to help those in spiritual or physical need. His mother was an activist of sorts, being one of the early members of the Women's Christian Temperance Union, the WCTU. (It is interesting to note that some problems persist in society in which women take an active role. In more recent times MADD, Mothers Against Drunk Driving, has gotten considerable attention.) The WCTU was concerned that drinking often destroyed families, and they wanted drinking banned altogether.

The Livingstons and Aldens liked Frank Hill right away, and he fit well into the group of friends and relatives. Grace and Frank decided that they would keep in touch through letters. Strangely, with this man it was hard to say good-bye. It was a feeling Grace had never had before.

Winter Park was still in the midst of summer when

the family returned home in August, but it was good to be back. Grace started planning her physical education classes for the coming school year.

The year went smoothly, and the family spent the following summer at Chautauqua. Grace wanted to spend more time with Frank Hill, and they had some wonderful times together. Grace also saw quite a bit of Frederick, and although she favored Frank in her mind, still Frederick was her dear friend and companion—from home. It was difficult to keep both men happy, but she enjoyed the challenge. Fortunately the men seemed to like each other and so the three of them often went places together, or in groups. Even so, by the end of the summer Grace felt even more drawn to Frank, and he to her.

The attraction of Frank over Frederick was not personality; clearly Dr. Starr was the more interesting "character." But Frank had deep spiritual interests and spoke more of heavenly things, while his competitor for Grace's heart spoke of the best and most interesting things this world had to offer. Grace had already set a pattern for her life that was not likely to falter, and she would most likely select the man who seemed more interested in the things of God.

The climax for this triangle came in Winter Park, without Frank Hill being present to state his case or defend his cause.

Word was received that both the Reverend Mr. Livingston and the Reverend Mr. Alden were being called to churches in the Washington, D.C., area. Grace, of course, would also move north with the family, since she was not supporting herself with her work at the college. It was inevitable that Grace and Frederick Starr would be separated by many miles.

Grace wrote a short letter of resignation to the president of the college, to which he replied:

Sept. 4, 1891

Dear Miss Livingston,

Your letter of the 18th Aug. has been received. I have reached home from the North only this week. Your going is a necessary part of much loss. It does not seem possible to fill your place, but some one must be set to do the best that can be done. Perhaps that person of whom you wrote may be the one for us. I am disposed to refer the matter to Mr. Lyman for a nomination. I should be unwilling to name anyone without previous consultation with him.

The prospect for the school is excellent. We need money for the furniture and heating plant. The $10,000 for the building has been subscribed and the work is making good headway.

I will write to Mr. Lyman this afternoon. I am favorably impressed with the person whom Dr.

Anderson recommends, all things considered. Give regards to all.

> *Very truly yours,*
> *Edward P. Hooker*
> (Rollins College Archives)

It was going to be hard to leave Winter Park and the students at Rollins. Grace had been active in the Christian Endeavor Society and the Bible study class at the school; they had studied the life of Christ together and had just begun a study on "Christ Among Men," by J. M. Mott, who was a teacher at Mr. Moody's school in Northfield.

It seemed that all the world knew that Grace and her family were leaving town. Every day people stopped them on the street to say how much they had enjoyed the friendship and how sorry they were that the Livingstons and Aldens were leaving.

September was almost over. Grace used the mornings for packing; in the afternoons she taught her gymnastic classes. It rained almost every afternoon and a cool breeze came out of the thunderheads as they passed by. The grass was "shockingly green" and the palms rustled in the breezes. Occasionally a giant thunderstorm would blow over the school and town, dropping torrents of water.

Grace had just finished working with her class on a wand drill one day when Frederick Starr came into the gymnasium. They had a date to play tennis that afternoon, but the courts were too wet to be played on. Students hovered around the door, waiting for a letup in the deluge. Each time the storm seemed to rest for a minute several students raced away to their dorms, dancing around the puddles in the sandy path. Within twenty minutes the students were all gone and Grace and Frederick found themselves alone in the artificial twilight, watching the storm from the doorway. They enjoyed the stillness for a minute or so and then Frederick turned and said quietly, "You don't have to leave, you know."

As Grace turned toward him, he held both of her hands very gently in his. She did not try to pull away. "I have to go, Frederick. My family is leaving," she said.

"You can stay here with me," he said. "Will you marry me?"

There was something about the mood that kept Grace from being surprised. The storm had passed. There was a dim glow of green from the wet trees, the gentle plopping of the rain on the sandy soil as it fell from the eaves of the building, and the thunder rumbling softly in the distance.

As serenely as the mood of the weather, she replied, "No, I can't marry you, Frederick. I love you as a friend, but I don't feel God has chosen us for each other."

"Are you in love with Frank?" he asked.

"I don't know, but maybe so."

"Can I walk you home?"

"That would be very nice."

The rain was falling very lightly and there was light in the eastern sky. It was a short walk to the Livingston house.

"Thanks for being so nice about my saying no, Frederick. You have such a wonderful mind and fine sense of humor that I know one day you will be a very important person. I shall always be happy when I hear of your success."

Frederick looked at her. It was difficult to speak but he managed to say, "Thank you, Grace. I have enjoyed your company very much."

"You still may." She smiled at him and walked onto the porch and into the house.

Frederick Starr went back to his room, gathered his books which were stacked around on the floor and packed them in trunks. He packed his clothing and personal effects. The following day he taught his classes as usual and, at the close of the class, left all his students' papers and his books on his desk. He paid all his bills in the town, including his rent. There was nothing left to do till morning.

At dawn a mule wagon arrived at Dr. Starr's quarters and his goods were loaded. Then he climbed aboard. The driver took him to the train station down the line from Winter Park where he caught the train to Orlando. From there he took the main line back north again.

What Dr. Starr did during the rest of 1891 is not

clear, but we can assume that he was at the Chautauqua meetings again the summer of 1892. Chautauqua had a university from 1883 to 1892, when it was discontinued. Dr. William Rainey Harper, who was on the staff, became the first president of the University of Chicago, and asked Dr. Starr to join him. He was a popular professor at the university for more than 30 years. In Dr. Starr's folder in the Department of Archives at Rollins College, a note was discovered. It was written by the late Dr. Frederick L. Lewton, one of his students at Rollins who later became one of the curators at the Smithsonian Institute: "Professor Starr left Winter Park very suddenly. Campus rumor was that his offer of marriage to Miss Grace Livingston, gymnasium instructor, was rejected."

A paper in the Rollins College file gives this summary of the life of Dr. Starr:

. . . . in 1892 he was called to organize the work of anthropology at the newly established University of Chicago, under William Rainey Harper. . . . During his thirty-one years there he was probably the most popular professor in the university. Though his classes were crowded,, and he was the only professor in his subject, he refused to add others, remaining, as he said "The Lone Star."

He had numerous personal idiosyncrasies. He refused to wear an overcoat, never used a telephone, and usually walked about the campus with an open book in his hands, while his apartment was a labyrinth of books stacked on the floors of various rooms. His frankness and fearlessness in the expression of opinion often made him enemies; on the other hand, his informality and camaraderie in the classroom created a loyalty seldom met with between students and professor. When he retired from the university in 1923 his former students presented him with a large purse, which enabled him to purchase a house in Seattle, Wash., a location convenient for his frequent trips to Japan.

Throughout his career he traveled widely for the sake of making anthropological studies. In preparation for the Louisiana Purchase Exposition at St. Louis, Mo., in 1904, he visited northern Japan and brought back with him a representative group of Aimu; he also visited various parts of the United States and Mexico, the Philippines, Korea, and Africa, returning several times to the last two. During these visits he lived the life of the people, and in Japan, at least, he wore the native dress.

Keenly interested in the intimate life of those he met, he was always inclined to take the part of minority or unpopular groups. While the world was condemning the African policy of King Leopold II, he visited the Congo and came forward with a vigorous defense of Belgian rule; while "imperialism" was at its height in America he advocated Philippine inde-

pendence. Mexico found in him an ardent advocate, and shortly before his death he defended Japan in the Manchukup dispute.

He was a chevalier of the Order of the Crown of Italy, a member of the Third Order of the Sacred Treasure of Japan, an officer of the Order of Leopold II (Congo), and had been awarded medals by Holland, Belgium and Liberia, as well as the palms of Officer of Public Instruction by the French government.

His greatest contribution to anthropology lies, however, in the wide interest he personally created in the subject, and in the appreciation of other peoples which he engendered in his students. In 1923 he went through the earthquake that devastated Tokyo and claimed many of his closest friends. Then years later he died of bronchial pneumonia in the same city. He was unmarried. . . ."

(From the Rollins College Archives and Dictionary of American Biography)

Grace followed the career of her friend Frederick Starr over the years. She had no regrets over not marrying him, but remained an admirer of his. She loved to learn and later she wrote and spoke about people and places almost as unusual and interesting as those Dr. Starr visited.

Preparation for the move north was in full swing and Grace packed with her things a half-finished manuscript which she vowed to herself she would finish in time for publication and release at Chautauqua that coming summer. On the train ride north from Florida to Hyattsville (near Washington, D.C.) Grace completed the manuscript.

Once settled in Hyattsville, home and church life went back to the pattern established in Winter Park, with Grace helping both her father and mother. Frank Hill came to visit almost at once. He was working on some postgraduate studies at Princeton but his friendship with Grace continued to develop by correspondence.

Frank lived by himself in a house provided by the church. It was neat and comfortable with three bedrooms, bath, kitchen, dining and living rooms. It also had a large front porch and a small garden at the back, with a carriage house at the rear of the property.

The relationship between Grace and Frank had grown to such a point by summer that it was arranged that the Livingstons would spend a weekend with Frank on their vacation, and that Charles Livingston would preach the Sunday sermon in Frank's church. Then the Livingstons planned to go on to New York to visit friends, and Frank would see them all again the following week at Chautauqua.

The congregation was delighted to meet the Livingstons, especially the young lady in whom Frank was interested. Many of them used Grace's syndicated Sunday school lessons and had read her books. They were impressed with the depth and insights of Charles's sermon. Frank's friends encouraged him to develop the relationship with Grace. He already knew he was in love, so the encouragement only spurred on his gentle pursuit.

Before the weekend was finished, he told Grace of his love for her. She was caught off guard for a minute, but it was no use denying that she was in love with him. She had thought about him so often that it had been a distraction to her writing, and it had kept her awake at night planning romance stories in her mind instead of Sunday school lessons! It was enough to make her cross at herself. So it was planned; he would give her a ring at Chautauqua that summer to announce their formal engagement.

In the summer of 1892, the family was back at Chautauqua and Grace's latest book had just been published. This review appeared in *The New York Evangelist*, February 5, 1892.

The Parkerstown Delegate *by Grace Livingston, author of "A Chautauqua Idyl," "A Little Servant," etc. 12 mo. Illustrated, 50 cents. At your bookstore.*

STORY

The Parkerstown Delegate *(Boston: D. Lothrop Company) is by Grace Livingston, and is written in the charming style for which this favorite author is noted. Her stories are too well-known to the readers of The Golden Rule to need special commendation by us. This story, because of its Christian Endeavour setting, will be of special interest to thousands of our readers. The way in which Lois describes the great Convention to little crippled Harley is capital, and the society that was formed out of what seemed at first rather unpromising material shows what may be done in many another Parkerstown. The scene with which the book closes, where the little crippled president, just before the Convention was to be held, went up to join the great convention that will never break up, as "the delegate from Parkerstown," is very touching. Few can read it without emotion, or close the book without breathing the prayer that many will follow in the footsteps of Lois and Harley and Franklin. The book is most attractively printed and bound, is illustrated by some charming pictures, and has a glittering silver Christian Endeavour badge on the cover.*

While walking Grace back to her cottage after the meeting that night, Frank again asked her to be his wife, and she accepted. He gave her a beautiful engagement ring, a large white diamond in a solitaire setting. Although it flashed in the moonlight very brightly, it was an inner glow that lighted their faces. That light of love between them was the reflection of a greater eternal love.

IN TUNE WITH WEDDING BELLS

CHAPTER VI

GRACE never kept a diary but she did keep a journal of sorts, a hodgepodge of information ranging from royalties received from her writings to newspaper clippings of interest to her. She also included notes she jotted down on sermons and poems that she liked. Poetry was a hobby with her. Here is one she typed and inserted in her journal in 1892.

THE BRIDAL VEIL

We're married, they say, and you think you have
won me.
Well, take this white veil from my head, and look on
me;
Here's matter to vex you, and matter to grieve you,

Here's doubt to distrust you, and faith to believe you,
I'm all as you see, common earth, common dew,
Be wary, and mould me to roses, not rue!

Ah! shake out the filmy thing, fold after fold,
And see if you have me to keep and to hold,
Look close on my heart—see the worst of its sinning,
It is not yours to-day for the yesterday's winning—
The past is not mine—I am too proud to borrow—
You must go to new heights if I love you tomorrow.

We're married! I'm plighted to hold up your praises,
As the turf at your feet does its handful of daisies;
That way lies my honor, my pathway of pride,
But, mark you, if greener grass grow either side,
I shall know it, and keeping in body with you,
Shall walk in my spirit with feet on the dew!

We're married! Oh, pray that our love does not fail!
I have wings flattened down and hid under my veil:
They are subtle as light—you can never undo them,
And swift in their flight, you can never pursue them,
And spite of all clasping and spite of all bands,
I can slip like a shadow, a dream, from your hands.

You, call me not cruel, and fear not to take me,
I am yours for my lifetime to be what you make me.
To wear my white veil for a sign, or a cover,
As you shall be proven my lord, or my lover;
A cover for peace that is dead, or a token
Of bliss that can never be written or spoken.

(In examining her papers it is sometimes hard to discover what was written by Grace and what was part of her collection of favorites. What was typed usually has been verified as her own work and we attribute this poem to her, but apologize if it is borrowed from someone else's work.)

In later years, Grace would often write of a girl being married in her grandmother's wedding dress and being given an heirloom ring, but at her own wedding everything was new. The dress was white satin with lots of lace. Real white flowers were fastened to the edge of the veil, and she held a bouquet of lilies of the valley. She was a pretty young woman, with a beautiful complexion and a sweet expression on her face. She had timeless beauty both without and within, and the combination of the tangible and intangible made her all the more striking.

The wedding was a family affair, with the Aldens living so near. The Reverend Mr. Alden gave the dedication prayer and Raymond, who was studying at Columbia University in Washington, D.C., where his parents lived, played the piano. The Aldens entertained the groom and several members of his family who came for the wedding.

The wedding day, December 2, 1892, was cold and clear. The plain, unimposing Hyattsville Presbyterian Church was beautifully decorated with flowers and a red runner.

(Many years later Grace and her girls were in the

Washington, D.C., area and the young ladies wanted to see the church where their mother was married. When they arrived, they found the building had been sold and was now a garage where automobiles were repaired. The girls teased their mother that she had been married in a garage and that the best man had probably been a Ford.)

At 6 P.M. friends wished farewell to the newly married couple at the train station, and they were off to Baltimore on their honeymoon. There they enjoyed concerts and plays in the evenings and museums and window-shopping during the days.

After their honeymoon, they went directly to western Pennsylvania to return to Frank's pastorate. Within a few minutes of their arrival, several neighbors stopped by with hot food and warm greetings. The church members planned a special wedding reception for them the following Sunday afternoon, and it was wonderful for Grace to see how devoted the congregation was to Frank.

It was an exciting time for them both, as they started establishing their home. Grace unpacked her things and started placing lace covers on the end tables and hand-made quilts over the blankets on the beds. Quickly the house was being transformed from a rough bachelor's quarters into a home with a woman's touch.

But within a month, Frank received a letter from the presbytery asking him to consider transferring to a larger church in eastern Pennsylvania. After a week of consideration and prayer, he wrote back accepting the new position at the Wakefield Presbyterian Church in Germantown, near Philadelphia. The church, with over two hundred members and nearly four hundred attenders in the Sunday school, had been without a pastor.

Within four months of moving into their first home, the young couple was on the train, moving all their things to suburban Philadelphia, and the process of settling in again and being welcomed by enthusiastic members was repeated.

The adjustment to married life came easily for both of the newlyweds, for each came from devoted and stable families. Grace was reminded of her father as she lived with Frank. He was interested in the same topics as Charles Livingston and was a good conversationalist, with an alert and studious mind. In fact, Frank Aydelotte, one of the presidents of Swarthmore College and a classmate of his at Washington and Jefferson College, called Frank Hill the most brilliant man in the class—the smartest one in their college during the four years they attended college together.

If Grace found life with Frank pleasant and easy to adjust to, she felt somewhat intimidated by his family. His father was powerful and aggressive, although he was loving and kind as well; and his mother was an energetic activist against the consumption of alcohol. Frank's brothers were as intelligent as he was, and successful in more lucrative professions. Sam, who later became a close friend and favorite of her children, was a medical doctor. He was head of the Pennsylvania State Mental Institution of Wernersville. Brother Frederic was president of an electric company; and their sister, Jessie, was married to a lawyer in Pittsburgh. It was hard for a small-town girl from modest means to keep pace with this crowd on the few occasions they all got together. Grace was a little awestruck the first few times she attended a Hill family gathering.

Grace and Frank seemed a perfect match. But with all the love, affection, and respect they shared, the marriage had one flaw. Grace was so loyal, and loved Frank so much that no one ever knew of any major problem in the relationship until twenty-five years after his death, and then she told only her children.

She had noticed within a day or two after the wedding that Frank seemed to have emotional swings. These were not violent ups and downs, but they did seem to have a pattern. Typically a day might start with Frank getting up in the morning, seemingly nervous and fidgety, but by breakfast he would be very calm, almost drowsy. Then, within a half hour or so, he would seem to adjust to the day and be his normal self. This pattern would repeat itself in the afternoon. Grace asked Frank why he was so fidgety and he replied, "That's just me."

One Sunday after Sunday school, Frank seemed uncharacteristically nervous and edgy. Grace asked if he was all right. He said that he was, but as he sat on the platform during the opening of the church service she could tell he was very uncomfortable. After the Lord's prayer and a hymn, he stood to give the announcements and following that he asked the song leader to come back onto the platform and lead in another song. Frank left the platform hurriedly and went into the annex of the building. Grace followed him, hoping to be of some help.

He entered his office and closed the door. Within seconds Grace followed, and what she saw when she opened the door surprised and disturbed her. Frank was in the process of swallowing something and he held another small tablet between his thumb and forefinger. His face contorted as he saw her standing there. He swallowed the second tablet and quickly picked up the bottle from the top of his desk and put it back into his coat pocket. Then he came to her and, with trembling hands, held her by the shoulders and whispered, "I've got to go preach. Pray for me! I'll explain everything later."

Grace was left standing there, her hands limp at her sides, deeply grieved and yet with no comprehension of what had happened. Was Frank seriously ill and hadn't told her? She wondered.

Frank walked back into the sanctuary just as the unscheduled hymn was coming to a close. He went straight to the platform and, when the hymn ended, he gave the sermon. He seemed a little tense at first but within a short time he seemed very relaxed. This Sunday his sermon was a bit shorter than usual, but, except for his "little attack," everything seemed all right.

As the pastor and his wife greeted people at the door, several people asked Frank if he were all right. "Oh, yes," he replied, and explained that he had a slight recurring illness that he was being treated for and occasionally he suffered an attack. This answer was accepted with sincere wishes for his complete recovery.

As they were walking home, hand in hand, Frank said, "I've tried to keep my problem from you, but I shouldn't have. I'm ashamed of myself but now I must explain."

"Are you seriously ill, Frank?" Grace asked, her eyes filling with tears.

"No," he said as they turned in at their gate. He walked with her into the house and sat on the couch in the living room. As he held her hand, Frank asked, "Do you remember that I told you how I used to have terrible headaches when I was at the university in Scotland?"

"Yes," she answered.

"Well, the doctor I went to there, a very highly recommended one, prescribed some medicine that helped a great deal. In fact, any time I got one of those headaches, I would take only one of those tablets and the headache would be gone within a few minutes. But, within about three months, I realized that I could not get along without the tablets. The doctors there don't tell you what they prescribe or I would have been more careful. He never warned me about the danger of the possibility of addiction."

"Addiction?" Grace barely whispered.

"Yes, to morphine. I've prayed about it. I've asked God to help me overcome it. I've confessed the sin of using it. But I can't stop." He went on, "Sometimes, like today, I try to put myself into a position that will embarrass me too much for me to leave and take one of those awful pills. I thought with you there that I could force myself to stop and that you would never have to know. But nothing works, Grace. Nothing."

Grace held his arm, crying. Neither of them spoke for several minutes. Then Grace got up. "I'll be right back," she said.

To Frank it seemed that Grace was back in just a moment, he had been so lost in thought. She placed a tray with bowls of hot soup, crackers, and cheese on the coffee table. She sat down again next to him and asked, "Will you ask the Lord to bless the food, Frank?"

Frank looked at her and realized she had washed her face, and it was hard to guess she had been crying just a few minutes before. The only sign was a little redness around her eyes. When Frank prayed, he thanked God for his wife first and then for the food He had provided.

Then Grace asked, "Who else knows about your problem?"

"I have told only my father, but I'm sure my mother also knows. No one else, except a doctor in Philadelphia. I asked if there were some way I could get over the desire for this drug. He said he didn't think so. In fact, he said in confidence that two physician friends of his in

New York have the same problem and that no one has found a cure. Grace, you don't know how guilty I feel sometimes and how helpless. But what can I do?"

"Frank, I love you. I don't know what I can do to help you, but I will if I can. You thought you were doing right; you thought you could trust your doctor in Scotland to do the best thing for you. Oh, Frank, you have such a good ministry here and God has certainly blessed your work; you can't feel guilt! Even the Apostle Paul had a problem he wrestled with and Jesus Himself suffered as a man and He was without sin. Keep praying and trusting. You're a wonderful husband and pastor."

Frank sighed. "I've spent years thinking about this and I feel that as long as I'm able, I will preach and teach God's Word and leave my personal problems in His hands. This horrible flaw in my life has helped me to understand the struggles and heartbreak in the lives of other people, and I'm sure I'm much more patient with people than I would have been had I not been plagued with this problem."

The minister and his wife continued to care for others, but the hidden sorrow that they shared stayed with Frank until death parted him from the weakness of his flesh. There was little understanding of addiction in the United States in 1892 and no rehabilitation centers existed.

Grace's reaction to Frank's problem is revealed to us by her only surviving child. "My mother never told us of our father's problem until twenty-five years or more after his death. She was so loyal to him. It was a terrible shock to her when she discovered that he could not get along without the drug. He wrestled against it in prayer and in every way that he knew. She was in terror when she saw him disappear from the pulpit a few moments before the service began. She knew he needed something to keep him going. This was a deep grief to her. No one knew how to get the best of it so they lived with it. It didn't hinder his desire to serve the Lord. He was considered a very successful pastor, and he preached deeply spiritual sermons. In spite of her deep sorrow when Frank died in his thirties, Grace felt that God had graciously taken him before worse disasters might have occurred."

Grace enjoyed her home and was known as a good cook to the many parishioners, friends, and relatives who visited. She seemed to have abundant energy. Squeezed in between the housework, magazine articles and Sunday school lessons flowed out in an ever-widening stream. Even when she was pregnant with her first child she didn't slow down her quest for new outlets for her writings. A pastor's income was low, and the payment Grace received from her work was a help to the young family.

On September 17, 1893, Margaret Livingston Hill was born. She was a tiny, plump, bright-eyed baby and a joy to the entire circle of family and friends. Marcia Livingston came and stayed with her daughter for the first few weeks to help with the housework and the baby.

She also provided inspiration and editorial help for her daughter's writings.

Cousin Raymond Alden was also an inspiration to Grace. Despite the seven-year difference in their ages, they were good friends. He was a few miles away studying at the University of Pennsylvania until he was graduated as valedictorian of his class, and with awards in English and Latin. In 1895 he taught English at George Washington University, and the following year went to Harvard where he received his M.A. degree. He was always close at hand and ready to discuss writing and publishers with Grace.

Even with her accelerated pace of life, Grace managed to write three more books before the turn of the century. *Katharine's Yesterday* was published in 1895; *In the Way* in 1897; and *Lone Point—A Summer Outing* in 1898. Each was brought out by a different publisher. The change in publishers has always confused readers. Up till this point, Grace had stayed with Lothrop as her book publisher. The reason for the change was not dissatisfaction. Each of these last three books had been published in serialized form in a magazine and the demand for bound copies was so great that each book had been offered by its magazine publisher. Later, between 1900-1920, she changed publishers for completely different reasons.

At home, Grace was teaching her precious and mischievous daughter, Margaret, who was almost five years old. Already she was reading well and playing simple pieces on the piano.

On January 24, 1898, Ruth Glover Hill, the second child of Frank and Grace, was born. Ruth was a quieter baby than her sister had been, but she was bright and quick-witted like her sister. Neither grew up to overshadow the other and they became close friends.

Grace was now thirty-three years old, with a well-established audience for her writings, yet she was still ten years away from her first major book and further yet from pioneering the modern Christian romance novel. But God was guiding her each step of the way. First her life and then her career would have dramatic changes forced upon them before her subject and style would mature.

ABOVE: *A family who loved to read together: Grace and daughter Margaret, her mother, Marcia, and her father, Rev. Charles Livingston.*

LOWER LEFT: *Grace Livingston Hill*

LOWER RIGHT: *Rev. Thomas Franklin Hill*

ABOVE: *D. Lothrop Co., regular publishers for Grace's mother and aunt, Marcia Livingston and Isabella Alden. With the assistance of her Aunt Isabella, Lothrop published Grace's first book when she was twelve years old.*

LOWER RIGHT: *Grace and daughters Margaret (left) and Ruth (right), at their daily family altar.*

TOP: *Margaret Livingston Hill and Ruth Glover Hill—lovely daughters of Frank and Grace.*

BOTTOM: *The home Grace designed and had built at 215 Cornell Avenue in Swarthmore, Pennsylvania.*

RIGHT: *Group picture taken at Panama Rocks, New York. Top: Margaret and a cousin, Sam Hill. Middle, right to left: Uncle Sam Hill (Frank's brother), Ruth, Tom Craig, F. J. Lutz (Grace's second husband), Boyd Craig, Uncle Hugh Craig, Aunt Jessie (Hill) Craig (Frank's sister), and Aunt Valeria Hill (Dr. Sam Hill's wife). Lower right: Uncle Fred (Frank's brother) and Aunt Margaret Hill, a friend of the family, and Grace.*

ABOVE LEFT: *Ruth Glover Hill, taken on the day of her high school graduation. The yellow daisies are from her boyfriend, Gordon Munce.*
ABOVE RIGHT: *Gordon and Ruth Hill Munce at the wedding of a friend.*
UPPER RIGHT: *Ruth Hill Munce*
LOWER RIGHT: *Robert Munce and his older brother, Gordon, Jr.*

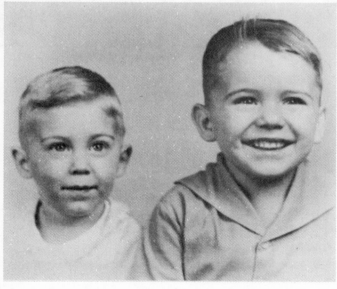

ABOVE: *"Baba" with Allyn (in small chair) and Marcia Walker, children of Margaret and Wendell.*

LOWER LEFT: *Grace Livingston Hill*

LOWER RIGHT: *Picture postcard Grace sent: "I've just stepped in to say 'Merry Christmas' to all, Lovingly, Grace."*

TOP: *Ruth Hill Munce holding her son "Barney" (a nickname for Gordon Munce, Jr.), with Grace, and Margaret Hill Walker. This photograph was taken in Grace's backyard.*

BOTTOM: *Grace signing a contract on the occasion of her one millionth book sold.*

THROUGH THESE FIRES

CHAPTER VII

THROUGH the years of being a minister's wife, life settled into a pattern. With great energy, Grace helped her popular and greatly admired husband in his church ministry. Together they visited the sick and sorrowing in their church and neighborhood, offering spiritual help. They rallied the church around the physical needs of the poor before the days of government-sponsored charity. Realizing that the word "charity" means "love," the people of the church offered help and loving concern for those in trouble.

Grace's love for young people was once again evident as she organized Bible studies and outings for the youth of the church. Often on Saturdays, young people, and even whole families, left from the pastor's house to go on hikes to nearby places of interest. Frank carried

Ruth on his shoulders, and Grace held Margaret by the hand. The teenagers carried the lunches and helped with the other young children. It was a noisy and happy group of fifty or more people who would spend the day enjoying each other's company. Each outing started with a prayer, and always there was a time during the day to reflect on the person of Jesus Christ—who He was and how a person could become acquainted with Him. Each person was reminded of his responsibility to worship, fellowship, pray, and give to others. These outings were times of growing together for church members and their pastor.

By early summer of 1899, Frank was having pain in his side. His doctor discovered that Frank was suffering from attacks of appendicitis. The doctor was very open with Frank, and told him that operating was very dangerous (which was true in those days); he suggested surgery only as a last resort. He advised Frank to eat a bland diet and to stay off his feet as much as he could. The family did not take a vacation that year, so he could rest and maintain his diet.

Frank was still able to preach most Sundays, but he had given up working at the church office or doing any visitation, which left Grace with extra responsibilities. By November, Frank was in such a bad state the doctor advised him to consider surgery. On November 15, Frank decided he must take the risk of an operation, for he felt he could not survive without it, no matter the risks of the surgery itself. On November 18, the operation was performed and the next day he was still in serious condition. The infection was widespread. Two days later his condition had worsened and he called for Grace and the girls. He told Grace that he did not think he would survive. He was so weak he could barely speak. The following day, November 22, 1899, the Reverend Thomas Franklin Hill went to live with his Lord.

Grace felt her life had been shattered. Yet she knew that in the bad, as well as the good, God had a purpose for each of His children. Still, life seemed very dark. It was a perplexing situation. She did not earn enough money from her writing to support the family. The house was the property of the church, so she had to find another home as soon as possible. The job market was bleak. There were few career jobs that would allow a woman to support a family, and Grace was not trained in any of them. Even if she could find a good job, who would take care of the girls?

The greatest pain was not the future with all its uncertainties, but the thought of a future without the love and support and companionship of Frank. Every time she thought of it, it seemed like a cold, black wave a hundred feet high was falling on her and crushing her soul.

In Grace's hour of great need, her mother and father were there to lean on. They had come to be with her when Frank decided to have surgery. The Aldens were not far away in Philadelphia, where Uncle Ross had been assigned a church. The family helped arrange the funeral service, which was held at the Wakefield Church. Raymond Alden wrote a memorial article about Frank, which appeared in the *Herald and Presbyter* magazine.

After the funeral, Grace's mother stayed with her and helped her look for a place to live. Grace decided that she wanted to live in a small town, so she and the girls could walk to everything; a town where there were good schools, including a good college. That way the children could stay home with her all through their schooling, and hopefully not be homesick as she herself had been in college. Higher education was becoming more and more important for girls, and she wanted to be sure that her girls were well-educated. Also, she felt a college town would have cultural advantages that might not be available elsewhere. With her plans laid, she searched the Philadelphia area, and finally decided that the town of Swarthmore was right for her.

The leaders in the church kept in daily contact with Grace and her mother, and they went with her to find a house and negotiate the rent. They were met in Swarthmore by Sam Hill, Frank's younger brother, who was very supportive and helpful over the years.

The house Grace rented was a pleasant three-bedroom, two-story wood frame structure on Harvard Avenue, one of the many streets in Swarthmore named after colleges.

Many friends came to help on moving day, but it seemed no one could comfort Grace that day. She just couldn't seem to stop crying. She would get control for a while, and then she would start weeping again. Grace had lived almost all her married life at the house in Germantown. She and Frank had loved each other so much, and now she wouldn't even be in the house that together they had made into a home. She knew that this was the final cutting of the earthly tie that had bound them together. Her grief was almost unbearable.

Grace seemed in a fog, listless; and her mother was worried about her. But Dr. Sam Hill assured Marcia Livingston that her daughter would recover within a few days and deal with her grief. Grace, he knew, would begin to cope before long. She was a strong personality and had many responsibilities. Necessity would force her to spend time with her family and her work.

Sam was right. Within the week, Grace was straightening up the house and showing the girls around the new town. At night she buried herself in work, writing articles and preparing for her next book. She was also keeping her eyes open for a house or a lot to buy, for she had received a sum from Frank's life insurance. Three thousand dollars! In those days that was considered a good amount, and it was enough to buy a modest house. Content that her daughter no longer needed her assistance, Marcia went back home with a promise that she would come whenever she was needed.

Writing was no longer a housewife's hobby that supplemented her husband's income. For Grace, it was now a necessity. It was the job in which a talented woman could excel and never leave her home. Grace needed to be home with her two young girls. She taught Margaret at home, giving her lessons and assignments to do while she sat and wrote. And what of two-year-old Ruth? Grace opened the door of the big closet in her study, put down a small rug and a blanket, and built a gate out of some slats of wood. The closet became a homemade playpen, where Ruth could play and see her mother. Grace wrote in short bursts of free time between the obligations of cleaning the house, cooking the meals, shopping, and keeping the girls occupied. Besides all these chores, she found time to help with the youth at the Swarthmore Presbyterian Church.

Grace now had to assume the role of both parents. She recognized that she was now spiritual head of the family, as well as the breadwinner. As soon as the days settled back into a normal pattern after Frank's death, the family devotions started again. For many years, a family prayer and Bible reading took place at least once a day. And she read Hurlbut's *Story of the Bible* over and over to the girls, before they learned to read.

Grace was always ready to comfort her children. Her daughter Ruth recalls an incident from her early years:

"One night I was in my crib, and I can remember how frightened I was of the dark. It was quiet, and I thought I could hear all manner of awful things coming to get me. When I cried out in fear, my mother came in and told me of the Shepherd Jesus, who was always with me. I was calmed and comforted. I never forgot that!"

Eighteen ninety-nine turned into 1900. A new century had begun. All the papers were filled with glowing reports of the new technical advances that were coming in the next hundred years. There was speculation that most Americans would be driving motorcars within the next fifty years. It seemed unlikely, but in this modern world, one never knows!

Grace, like her father and late husband, was interested in news and current events. But she was too busy to theorize about the 1900s. What needed to be done, with utmost haste, was to finish her new book. By February, her latest effort was complete—*A Daily Rate*, published by The American Sunday School Union.

In early June, a family vacation was planned. The Aldens had found a cottage at Point Pleasant, New Jersey, for the summer, and the Livingstons and the Hills came to stay for a week. It was so good to be together again. Raymond had written some prize-winning stories and Pansy and Grace each had a new book just coming out. They read to each other selections of their newest projects, making comments and helping each other with development of characters and plot. There was also time for discussion of theology and politics. For recreation, they played a lot of tennis, took long walks, fished, and saw the local sights. It was a delightful, relaxing time. Each of them returned home rested, thanking God for their wonderful family and fellowship.

Marcia Livingston often wrote to her daughter to encourage her, and she loved to get news of her grand-daughters. Marcia still liked to look over her daughter's manuscripts before they were sent off to the publisher. But by the end of June, the once-a-week letters had lost their relaxed tone, and were filled with concern over Charles' health.

During June, Charles was bedridden, and his condition was described as an abdominal obstruction. There was no medical knowledge on how to operate for such a condition. The doctors said that all they could do was to try to make him as comfortable as possible.

Then her mother wrote: "If you don't come at once, you probably will not see your father alive again." So on July 1, Grace went to Hyattsville with the girls to be with her mother, and to visit her father for the last time. Oh, how she prayed that God would spare her father. This was the man by whom she measured all others, and the family needed him so much. What would her poor mother do without him? What was God's purpose in all this sorrow?

Charles was happy to see her. Although in pain and barely able to speak, he asked to see his grandchildren. The visit on the second of July lasted only ten minutes, for he was too weak to respond or to keep his eyes open. Marcia and Grace took turns staying with him, day and night.

Church members looked after the children and brought food for the family, helping in any way they could. Uncle Ross and Isabella arrived on the fourth to give whatever assistance they could. By then Charles was in a coma. He died on July 6, 1900.

Family members and friends helped Marcia pack her things, and within two weeks, she was living in Swarthmore with Grace. It was a difficult time for them both, but soon Marcia was insisting that Grace divide the household work with her. Each had their chores around the house, plus teaching and looking after the children.

CHAPTER VIII

IF THE CENTURY dawned bleak for Grace Livingston Hill, it also dawned productive. After spending Christmas with the Aldens, Grace and her mother settled in at Swarthmore to their jobs of raising the children, doing church work, and writing.

Grace was prolific; she wrote articles, Sunday school lessons, and books. In 1902, she produced *The Angel of His Presence*, *The Story of a Whim*, and *An Unwilling Guest*. The following year, two books were published: *According to the Pattern* and *Because of Stephen*.

Over the past fifteen years, she had written thirteen books, and there had never been more than a two-year gap between them. Eight of those books had been written in the past six years. But not another book was written until 1907. What happened to the prolific writer who was developing so nicely and who needed to sell her work to support her family?

Actually a flurry of activity was going on. Grace was fighting a spiritual battle with depression to be sure, but she was finding victory in prayer and Bible study. The children were getting older and she was still teaching them at home. Besides her syndicated column, she was writing short stories for *The Christian Endeavor World*, the American Sunday School Union, Golden Rule Press, and the *Washington Star* (her syndicated column publisher). Besides these, she was also contributing to *Our Sunday Visitor*, published in England. Both adults were working actively in the Swarthmore Presbyterian Church in women's groups and Sunday school.

Grace was also thinking about two completely different objectives. One was her plan for her own house. She had always dreamed of having a lovely place of her own. She studied pictures and made sketches of the kind of house she wanted. She even produced a small painting as an exercise to get her thoughts together in preparation for this major project. The second objective was to change her style of writing so completely that she would appeal to non-Christians as well as Christians. But she intended to have a clear gospel message in her books.

The first goal started to become a reality when she purchased a lot on Cornell Avenue, around the corner from her rented house. In 1904 she had a modest house built on the lot.

To get the house she wanted, she needed more money, and to earn more, she needed a wider reading public. She sought advice as to how to proceed. After much discussion with friends and reading literary magazines, she decided to try a western. Zane Grey westerns were becoming very popular at this time. The problem was, she had never been west of Pennsylvania. She developed a story plot but lacked a setting. She could research a state, but still she felt that she could not adequately describe the people or the setting at a level of quality that would be convincing to readers. Not only was this a new type of writing for her, but she was determined that this book would be the best she had ever written.

She ran an ad in several newspapers in western states for someone to help an author describe a western setting. Each reply was followed up with a letter of thanks and one question to be answered: "Please describe the sitting room in your own house." She judged the replies on detail and vividness of description. Within two months she had chosen her helper. She quickly began to develop a friendship and acquire a well of information she needed for the opening chapters. So the book *The Girl from Montana* was born.

The girls were old enough by now to be interested in the work their mother was doing, and both of them were enrolled in school. Each evening when they returned home, they eagerly read the latest chapters. Often Ruth and Margaret stood behind their mother as she typed her manuscript, and read as the story came pouring out of her fingertips and magically onto the paper. Grace dedicated the book "to Miss Virginia Cowan of Cowan, Montana, whose bright, breezy letters aided me in the writing of Elizabeth's experiences in the West."

After the book was published, fan mail poured in from the West with expressions of amazement at the accuracy of detail in the setting of the story. *The Girl from Montana* was her biggest success yet. The goal for a larger readership had been reached.

Grace was not yet satisfied. She wanted to find another publisher, one that had been established for many years and had the resources to promote her books. She also wanted a rapport with an editor who could guide her into better markets, and would take enough interest to help her develop into a better author. Another essential requirement, she felt, was that the new publisher would allow her to include in each of her works the message of God's salvation for mankind through Jesus Christ. It was a tall order but, as usual, she was willing to work to see it happen. At family prayer time each night, the family asked for guidance for Grace in her writing and in choosing a publisher.

Even while writing the western, Grace was looking for a subject for her next book. A newspaper columnist friend suggested that historical novels were becoming very popular, and she might want to try one.

The suggestion seemed a good one and she discussed the possibility with her mother. Without hesitation, Marcia Livingston said she had just the story. To Grace's surprise, her mother told her an elaborate tale that had taken place in their family in the 1830s, a few years before she was born.

As Grace took notes, her mother made two other important suggestions. One was to visit Aunt Margaret Cady Livingston, who was almost a hundred years old. She was still in good health and mentally sharp. The second suggestion was to contact Cousin Henry. He was the well-known artist, E. L. Henry, who specialized in depicting Americana of the 1830s. (Later his art became a part of historic record, and hangs in many museums and galleries in America today, including five works at the Smithsonian Institute in Washington, D.C.)

Grace at once made arrangements to go to Johnstown, New York, where Aunt Margaret was living with the Frank Miller family. Grace's mother and the two young girls went along. Aunt Margaret had been born in Johnstown in 1809. She had moved to New York City in the 1850s, but had returned to Johnstown to retire. She was the sister of Eliza Livingston Lynde, whose husband was a New York Senator for many years.

"Aunt Margaret" was greatly loved by relatives and friends and Grace had named her elder daughter after her. Even though confined to a chair on the porch during good weather, Aunt Margaret had many visitors. She not only remembered the story in detail, but could also describe the setting in which the story took place. With mental energy and considerable physical stamina, Aunt Margaret dedicated several hours to the telling of the story. On the following two days, she described whatever scene Grace envisioned for her book. In fact, Aunt Margaret insisted that Grace and her family stay as long as it took to complete the task.

When the work was finished, Grace thanked Aunt Margaret and promised to dedicate the book to her. "No, Gracie," she said. "I have only told you a bit of family history. You should dedicate your book to someone who has helped make you what you are. For my sake, dedicate your book to Charles."

Armed with her notes from Aunt Margaret, Grace was ready to see Cousin Henry. She wrote a note and invited him to dinner. During the meal they discussed the book. Afterwards the whole family got involved in a discussion about the clothing and life-style of the 1830s. Uncle Henry drew some sketches for the girls—one of a parasol and another of a horse-drawn carriage wheel. Both were in magnificent detail. He sketched while he carried on a conversation as if he were doing nothing else.

The second meeting with Cousin Henry to discuss the book took place at the studio in his home. There Grace saw drawings and paintings of buildings, people in the costume of early days, boats, ships, and early steam locomotives and machinery. Here was a wealth of information for descriptive detail. "If it will help at all, I will be glad to do five or six pen-and-ink drawings for your book," suggested her cousin. Grace was delighted, and asked him to do at least one as soon as possible so that she could "take it around to the publishers, so they can see the whole concept of the book."

Here, she felt, was her best chance yet—a terrific story with many accurate details, and top-quality illustrations by an artist with a reputation as an expert in the period of history about which she wanted to write. But just to be sure, she took the train into Philadelphia and researched both the period of time in American history and the area in New York where the story took place. Fortunately, Philadelphia had one of the finest libraries in the country, and she made good use of it. She also visited museums in the area, analyzing period items. This was a family project in which the girls and her mother took part. Once the research was complete, Grace was like a cataract after a heavy rain upstream. It seemed the words poured onto the paper like an unleashed river on a floodplain. Day and night the literary tide flowed. Within five weeks from the time she sat down to start writing, the first draft was finished.

During this time of intense work, the girls were never neglected. Grace often stopped in midsentence to answer a question from one of the children. Usually when the girls came home from school, she would stop her work and be with them; then, only after they had gone to bed, would she start her work again.

The story takes place in upstate New York, and the scenes are laid in the early part of the 1800s. Two sisters of completely different temperaments and two young men of equally contrasting character are chiefly involved in the plot.

Kate Schuyler, the eldest sister—flashy, self-willed, and the "life of the party"—is about to be married to handsome and wealthy David Spafford, although she does not love him. On the night before the wedding, Kate elopes with Captain Leavenworth, a former boy-friend. Next morning, the family is assembled and the wedding guests are arriving. No bride! Kate's father, deeply apologetic to David Spafford, suggests that to save the Schuyler reputation and to save face for David, perhaps he would accept the younger daughter, Marcia. Dazed with shock, he reluctantly accepts, and young Marcia, at age seventeen, is married the next day in her sister's wedding dress!

The honeymoon trip is none too pleasant for Marcia, knowing that her husband is brokenhearted and still in love with her sister. But Marcia has loved David secretly almost since they met, and so she tries to build a loving relationship, even though the marriage was a last-minute attempt to save family honor. Gradually, David's affection changes from fondness for Marcia as a good-natured child who can cook and sew and play the piano for him to that of the proper love of a man for his wife.

Later Kate tries to regain control of David for her

own social and material advantage. She does not succeed, however, for David now understands the true love he has found in Marcia.

The crowning touch of the story is the real bridal trip after David and Marcia have awakened to their true feelings toward each other. The bridal trip is made on the first run of the DeWitt Clinton, the first locomotive engine ever to run on the Albany Railroad—and at the breathtaking speed of thirteen miles per hour!

One of the skeptics in the story "did not believe that an engine would be able to haul a train any appreciable distance whatever." He believed that he had come out to witness the entire company of "fanatics" being circumvented by the "ill-natured iron steed that stood on the track, surrounded by gaping boys and a flock of quacking ganders, living symbols of the people who had come to see the thing start." Whether they were disappointed, every child in school knows.

The book is a fine story and a study of the customs of another age in America, taking place just at the advent of the steam locomotive.

As soon as the work was completed, Grace put one of Henry's pen-and-ink drawings in her portfolio, and made an appointment to "see someone in your editorial department" at J. B. Lippincott Company, the old and prestigious Philadelphia publishing house.

When she arrived, she was introduced to Mr. J. Bertram Lippincott, Sr. Grace was surprised when he invited her into his private office. He was very receptive to

her ideas about the book. After looking over the manuscript for about ten minutes, he told her that she had
great promise; and that he would commit his firm to
taking the book, if she would promise to give him an op-
tion on a sequel to *Marcia Schuyler*. So it was agreed,
and a contract was drawn up.

Grace went home elated, for many breakthroughs
had been made that day. Each member of the family
thanked God for the progress made.

During the next two weeks Grace was getting her
thoughts together for the sequel. Then she got a note
requesting that she come to see J.B. again. This time
the meeting was not as pleasant; however, J.B. was the
perfect gentleman, and a person one could trust impli-
citly. He was always honest and straightforward with
everyone. After he made Grace comfortable, he told her
that he wanted to talk to her about personal success as
an author. J.B. looked across at her from behind his
mahogany desk piled high with manuscripts, and in
kindly, schoolteacher fashion, gave his new author a
lecture on worldly success as a novelist. His message
was simple. "No more preachy Sunday school stuff in
your manuscripts." Reason: "It won't sell to the wider
audience that you are now ready to reach. Good moral
principles, good winning over evil, all those things are
fine. But no gospel!" He handed back her manuscript
and told her to make the necessary revisions, and then
resubmit it.

It was a hard blow. What would God want her to do?

How would this conflict be resolved? She had signed a contract for two books; she would have to honor it. But after that, there would have to be a strategy employed that would make all her goals a reality.

When the book was published in 1908, a copy was sent to Aunt Margaret. Printed just before the index of illustrations was a dedication: "To the dear memory of my father, The Rev. Charles Montgomery Livingston, whose companionship and encouragement have been my help through the years." The memory of her father's love and help still remained, and was still an inspiration to her long after his death. (It is a tribute to her father that Grace, now gone many years, still has a living testimony and ministry around the world; "He/She being dead yet speaketh.")

Marcia Schuyler was a big success, and the publishers certainly did a fine job of promoting the book. Lippincott had a newspaper clipping service, and the book got favorable reviews from over one hundred newspapers throughout the country. One reviewer wrote that just having the book for its artistic appeal was worth the price of $1.50. The book was beautifully done, with a full-color picture on the dustcover, and the same illustration on the cloth cover of the book itself. It had a brown field with roses scattered over it, like fancy wallpaper. Just above the center line of the book was a picture frame with a portrait of Marcia Schuyler.

The inside artwork had six excellent drawings by E. L. Henry, and there was a full-color frontispiece by

Anna Whelan Betts. The title page was done in two colors. It was a fine production and confirmed Grace's feelings that she had been led to the right publishers and that somehow God would also work a way for her to have a strong ministry to accompany her success.

It was the beginning of a long and friendly relationship. She liked "J.B." and he obviously liked her, although they did have a few ups and downs until about 1920. After that, all her books were done in first edition by Lippincott.

BLUE RUIN

FIVE years before the publication of *Marcia Schuyler*, Grace was struggling to make a living for her family and she was still teaching her two girls at home. Even though she was very busy, Grace was lonely. She thought about the possibility of marriage again.

Flavius Josephus Lutz came on Sundays to Swarthmore from Germantown to play the organ for the Swarthmore Presbyterian Church. He lived with his parents, and taught a few music students at their home. He was a salaried minister of music at the church. He was an excellent musician by natural talent, and he had also had fine training.

Although she did not play a musical instrument herself, Grace had started her girls on music lessons at age five. Margaret had been studying piano for five years and Ruth for six months. F.J. showed keen interest in their progress and gave helpful advice.

A friendship developed between F.J. and Grace during the year of 1903, and F.J. proposed marriage early in 1904. He was twenty-four years old and she was thirty-nine.

Grace was flattered by the proposal from this talented young artist and asked for time to think it over. She discussed the possibility with several close friends, and almost all of them advised her not to marry. Still, it seemed right. A husband, a father, and music teacher for her daughters, a person who loved beauty as much as she did . . . she considered it all and said, "Yes."

At once her writings were published under the name Grace Livingston Hill-Lutz, and for several years she wrote under that name.

F.J. was a pleasant-looking man, slim and balding. The fringe of curly hair on the sides was short, but in back it was long and thick, reaching down to his collar. Grace preferred men to wear their hair medium length, as her father had, although neat short-trimmed haircuts were in style in 1904.

Within a few weeks, life became strained with F.J. He took no leadership role in the home, and contributed nothing to the running of the household. In fact, he had little work to do, and he didn't seem to know how to go about getting a job. Grace organized a music school for him, and let people know that her husband taught music. F.J. was pleased to have music students, and the house was used as a music studio as well as a writer's study and a home. Still, he never contributed anything to the household expenses.

The year after her second marriage, Grace enrolled her children in school for the first time. Margaret was ten and she started in the sixth grade. Ruth was almost seven and she started in the second grade.

It wasn't long before other flaws in the new husband's character started to show themselves. F.J. seemed to need someone to criticize, someone to degrade. He needed an enemy. Really, he tried to be fair about it, because everyone got a turn!

The dinner table became, as it were, a cockpit with the rooster attacking the hens. He started with the grandmother, Marcia Livingston. She was strong enough to defend herself, but it was very unpleasant. These episodes would start with suspicious questions, such as, "Mrs. Livingston, why are you always speaking against me when my back is turned?" Another time he might start the opening round with, "Grandma, you certainly are clumsy. Every time I walk near the kitchen you seem to be breaking something. Don't you think you ought to let someone else look after the dishes?" Marcia Livingston, not to be intimidated by this young upstart, would attempt to defend herself.

F.J. did a fine job of teaching Margaret. She became very accomplished at both the piano and the organ. But when it was Margaret's turn to be his target, even being a model student was not good enough. He started by picking on her music and, later on, any boys that came to visit her. "You don't know how to pick friends wisely, do you?"

There are times when even a bully gets a black eye from a victim. F.J. was not dealing with weak women, and sometimes he was outwitted and trapped in his own arguments. On other occasions the women banded together and countered his verbal attacks to such an extent that he would run off to his bedroom and not come out all day except for his meals. At these times, there was little or no table conversation. He would not speak to any of them for as long as a week at a time. But, to his music students, or to his visitors, he was the perfect gentleman.

F.J. Lutz remained a spoiled child all his life. If he distressed the family, he also amused them with his misbehavior.

If he disapproved of the company that was invited to the house, he would show his displeasure by going into the bathroom that was on the second floor above the living room, running the water in the tub full force, and thumping on the floor. At other times he would go into the basement, below the living room, throw wood around, and swear. He did fairly well at throwing wood against the floor and walls, but had never developed swearing to a very proficient level. Since he spent most of his time around the house and the church, is it any wonder he had only a two-word vocabulary to curse with? "Devil damn! Devil damn!" he would fume at the top of his high tenor voice. No wonder he was frustrated.

Years later, the family could laugh about some of the antics, and tease each other about the excuses they made to cover the embarrassing noises coming from the second floor or the basement, depending on where F.J. had decided to throw his tantrum.

These were dark days for Grace. She knew she had made a terrible mistake, and yet divorce did not enter her mind. She had made a lifetime commitment before God, and she felt very strongly that she should keep that commitment. She tried to create a happy atmosphere for the family. During this time she also continued writing.

The year before her second marriage, Grace bought a new desk, which she used until 1936. It was ingeniously made. It had an ornamental railing along the far side of the top to keep papers from sliding off the desk. It had three drawers on each side of the foot well, and a panel in the desk top itself that folded to resemble the top of a lectern. This made a perfect holder on which to set corrected manuscripts for retyping. Her upright, open-sided Remington typewriter sat just in front of this manuscript holder. Hooked to the side of the desk was a nine-inch ledge, held in place with pegs. This was used as a bookshelf or a place to stack papers. Attached to the back was a wooden rack where books or files could be stored. Later, for comfort, she bought a secretary chair of matching mahogany, with casters and adjustable back.

One of Grace's shortcomings was that she was a worrier. The children used to tease her that if she did not have something to worry about, she would be miserable. Yet she had absolutely unshakable faith in the faithfulness of God. Prominently tacked to her desk was a small aluminum plaque quoting John 14:1: "Let not your heart be troubled." That little plaque stayed on her desk for many years. It was a lesson she was letting God teach her.

Life with Mr. Lutz continued to be difficult, although there were bright spots when he would be very charming, and the whole family would have fun together on outings with young people. Many young people came to the house for counseling and to see the girls. Grace was always there, ready to be a mother, counselor, or just a friend.

One Friday morning F.J. left the house and did not return by nightfall. After hours of worry and telephoning, Grace finally located him at his parents' house. He came home the next day. This pattern continued. Sometimes he didn't show up for his music classes. Then his truancy extended to the Sunday morning church services where he was expected to play the organ. Margaret would fill in for him, but it was very embarrassing to the whole family to have to make excuses for him.

When he left home he always seemed to go to his parents' house. After a while, Grace didn't call there any more; he would come home when he was ready. After a particularly lengthy time away from the family, Grace, after much thought and prayer, confronted him with the facts and told him, " . . . please don't come back." She hoped that this would cause him to ask forgiveness or to make some positive response, but instead he seemed rather relieved. He only came back for a visit or two after that. He left in May of 1914.

Sixteen years after Mr. Lutz left her, Grace received a letter from a casual acquaintance addressing her Mrs. Lutz. Her reply summarizes her feeling of that era in her life:

May I call your attention to my name, please. It is not "Lutz" but "Hill." Mr. Lutz went away over fifteen years ago after causing us ten years of very great unhappiness, and when I found that without legal procedure I could legally retake my former name which was also my children's name I was glad to avail myself of the privilege. I have not used the name on my books for a number of years but possibly you have happened to notice it on my older books, and thought the other was a nom de plume, though it is Hill now on even the old reprints.

It is not of course a matter of great importance, only that I like my friends to know I am Mrs. Hill. Of course it is not a thing I talk about much. . . .

Her publisher had advised her to remove the name Lutz from her books because the feeling against Germany was very strong during and after the First World War. They felt that over a period of time, it would not be good for sales. She was happy to oblige them for personal reasons.

Once, while on a trip through the New England countryside, Grace saw a whole hillside covered with beautiful blue flowers. She asked her friend, who was driving the car, to stop so she could get a better look.

"What kind of flower is it?" she asked.

"Blue Ruin," was the reply. "It just takes over, and nothing else can grow. It ruins everything."

It reminded Grace of her own life over the period of her second marrriage. Blue Ruin! Her friend's remarks planted a seed, and provided the title and theme for the next novel.

THE HOUSE ACROSS
THE HEDGE

CHAPTER X

GRACE longed for a home of her own, one that could be added to or altered as she wished. After three or four years in the rented house on Harvard Avenue, she was eager to build. With the little money that was left from Frank's insurance, and what she had earned from her writing, she had enough for a modest home.

It was a small stone house, with three bedrooms, built in a wooded area just around the corner from the rented house. When it was built on Cornell Avenue in 1904, it was the only house on the block. That little house was a delightful challenge to Grace, and over the years it grew to be a large fourteen-room home, with beautiful stone arches and plenty of room for the family and a variety of uses.

Grace's house became a focal point for family life and activities. It was a home for her children and her mother, and it was a studio where she could write. It was also a lovely and comfortable setting where she could counsel and encourage young people. The house also functioned as a music school, which her daughters directed after Mr. Lutz left.

The house, however, was more than a functional place for work and social activities. It was another art form in which Grace could indulge. She had a deep desire to design her own house. A friend of the family was an architect and builder, and Grace asked him to do the add-ons and alterations.

Around the dinner table, he gave advice on design and drew a sketch of a rather conservative and conventional L-shaped building. It was not interesting enough for Grace. The harsh lines of an L-shape must be broken by rounded corners and curved porches, accessible through large French doors. And, because she loved stone arches, a number of them must be incorporated into the design. She argued with her architect about a tree which he thought should be removed because it was in the way of a proposed front porch. Grace wanted to leave the tree and incorporate it into the design of the porch. He demurred strongly; it would make the whole design look awkward and ugly. Grace invited him back the following evening to discuss it further.

"I want to show you something," she said when he arrived, and she led him into the dining room. She had spent most of the previous night building a cardboard model of her dream home. "I am showing you the end result," she said. "You need to help me get there a step at a time." She had a kind of courage that made her keep on striving toward her goals. She got the architect's enthusiastic approval, and the house progressed to her liking.

The finished house was lovely and restful to the eyes. The gray granite stones sparkled in the morning sunlight from myriads of tiny mica flakes. The stonework of the porch, especially around its arches, was draped with dark green climbing ivy. The porch itself was paved with large red tiles, and the heavy oak front door had a large brass knocker.

A prominent feature of the house was a large tower, about halfway back on the north wall. It was built of granite fieldstones mortared together. Six steps on the outside of the tower led to a beautiful arch in which a pair of white-painted French doors opened invitingly into the far end of the living room. A large window was set in the second floor of the tower. The top was level with the third floor of the house, and formed a porch, with embrasures, like a fort or the top of a castle wall.

In the front hallway, a large mirror was hung just opposite the front door, with a small mahogany table and an umbrella stand to the side. Three doorways led out of the hallway. To the left was the living room, straight ahead was the dining room, and to the right a stairway rose to the second floor and an archway led to the family room.

The family room was appropriately called "The Stone Room" with interior walls of rough-hewn fieldstone. Natural light filled the room from the large arched windows. The gray stone walls were offset by the red terracotta tile floor. Low hot-water radiators ran all along the right side of the room, from the French doors to the wall at the end. A long built-in bench over the radiators, covered with green velour cushions, provided a warm place to sit on a cold day. The fifteen-by-thirty-foot room, with a large fireplace at the end, was a cozy retreat in winter. The high ceilings, wide windows and extra tall doors kept the room cool and pleasant on warm days. A long, narrow Persian carpet ran down the center of the room, but the furnishings were casual.

The living room was somewhat more formal, with overstuffed couches and large wingback chairs arranged in two groupings. Elegant antique Persian cushions were scattered on couches and chairs. A large Kazakh Persian carpet, in shades of blue and cream, covered the floor.

What appeared to be a tower on the outside of the house was an extension of the ground-floor room. Set into the semicircle of the tower, on a hardwood floor, was a grand piano. Across from it, in the main part of the room, stood a baby grand. Music stands and stringed instruments in cases were placed here and there, and a mahogany rack, containing hundreds of pieces of classical sheet music, stood in the corner.

This was a room in which to relax, to be entertained, and to enjoy fine music.

The dining room had large windows and a porch at one end. A large sideboard stood along one wall. A built-in china cabinet shared the wall opposite the windows with a built-in seat about six feet long, hinged to form convenient storage for winter boots. A very large mahogany table stood on a Persian rug in the center of the room. With extra leaves, the table could seat twenty-two people.

Silver candlesticks and flowers always adorned the table, most often roses from the garden where many varieties bloomed all spring and summer. At mealtimes, water was poured from a sterling silver pitcher, covered with beads of condensation when filled with ice water in the summertime. Silver napkin rings, each with a family member's initials engraved upon it, held linen napkins.

Guests were served on blue and white Spode Geisha or Black Knight china. A meal for guests often included a large roast of beef, with Grace or, later, one of her sons-in-law standing to carve at the table. When everyone was served, a family member or a guest was asked to thank God for the food. Grace wanted everyone to remember that it was God Himself who had poured out material blessings upon them, and they should not forget to thank Him often.

Grace's bedroom-study was located on the second floor of the house, and almost all of her books were written there. The room opened onto an uncovered porch; and sometimes in good weather she did some writing out there.

To the right of the entrance stood a single bed, and just beyond it a day couch was built in under the casement windows. On the opposite wall were her clothes closet, a door opening onto the porch, and the door to her private bath. The focal point of the room was an eleven-by-thirteen-foot Chinese carpet, kept bare, perhaps so Grace could enjoy its beautiful colors and design. At the far end of the room, her desk was positioned on one side of a fireplace, and a large, blue velour armchair and footstool on the other.

Just outside Grace's bedroom was a large sitting room where she kept her library of reference books and a set of her own works. It was a cozy private family room, with three other bedrooms opening onto it.

The third floor of the house was a self-contained apartment, with bedroom, bath, and kitchenette, as well as a large playroom (about fifteen by thirty feet) which doubled as a guest room. An open porch, on top of the tower, adjoined the third floor.

For many years, a fine clay tennis court covered most of the backyard, so that her girls and other young people would have a place to enjoy themselves.

However, as much as Grace enjoyed adding a new room here and a bay window there, she valued home more than house, family more than fame, and God's blessing more than a good bank balance.

BIG BLUE SOLDIER

M R. LUTZ left Grace only two weeks before her younger daughter Ruth graduated from high school in 1914, at the age of sixteen. His departure brought about another change in Grace's life. Adjusting to his absence seemed to rejuvenate her, however, and with boundless energy she happily pursued a number of new horizons.

Grace accepted many out-of-town speaking engagements, and traveled throughout the Northeast, autographing her books at leading bookstores. It seemed that she wrote her three books a year in her "spare" time. Always she had a new story developing before the book she was currently working on had been completed.

Then, there was the house. She was always planning another addition—a room here, a turret there, an open porch, a cupboard, or a rose garden. These were some of the projects that kept this woman, in her mid-fifties, occupied eighteen hours a day, seven days a week.

Fortunately, Grace's children were able to keep pace with a high standard of academic achievement at Swarthmore College and a full social calendar. The music school, which they were already running, began to grow, and both girls were serious music students. The energy they exhibited was second only to their mother's.

Gordon Munce, whose family lived just a few blocks away from the Hill house in Swarthmore, had known both of the girls since their days in Christian Endeavor Society. He and Ruth became close friends at Swarthmore College, and the relationship developed into a romance over a period of several years.

During the summers of 1914 through 1916, between college terms, Gordon traveled with the Chautauqua Circuit, a religious and cultural extension of the main Chautauqua Conference in New York. The group traveled to small towns throughout the East and Midwest, bringing excellent speakers and music to communities which otherwise would be deprived of such cultural activities. Its promoter and president was Dr. Paul M. Pearson, a professor at Swarthmore College who later became governor of the Virgin Islands. His son Drew and Gordon were good friends, and both worked on the Chautauqua tent crews. Later Drew Pearson became a well-known radio news commentator.

In addition to setting up tents and chairs, Gordon was

given bit parts in some of the operas the group performed. In later years, one of his favorite stories was about an incident which occurred at one of the opera performances.

The star performer was a woman of surprising birth. She was a dying heroine in the opera. In the final scene, she sat up in a coffin and, along with full orchestral accompaniment, gave her last good-bye in her full, soprano voice. When the coffin lid was closed, the pallbearers came to carry her out. One evening Gordon and another performer were carrying the coffin down three steps to the ground in the backstage area, when the young performer slipped and dropped his end of the coffin. The heroine threw back the lid and, with anger sharpening the edge of her fine soprano voice, shrieked her outrage in words normally associated with irate drill sergeants. Unfortunately, through the thin walls of the tent, the audience heard the full outburst.

Grace always relished the recounting of such incidents in the lives of her beloved young people.

It was the beginning of World War I, and many of the young men Ruth and Margaret had known in high school and college were drafted into the army for service overseas. Both girls were busy with the music school and both were studying music privately.

Ruth traveled by train to New York City every two weeks to study violin with Theodore Spiering, who was considered at that time to be the finest violin teacher in America. When the war ended, many German musicians contacted Mr. Spiering, hoping to sell their musical instruments. These performers desperately needed American dollars because the deutsche mark had become virtually valueless; to some, selling a violin, a cello, or some other stringed instrument meant survival.

Mr. Spiering went to Germany and purchased instruments for his students. He not only helped provide the German musicians with spendable currency, but he also helped bring to the United States an influx of fine-quality old-European instruments.

For Ruth Hill, he purchased a beautiful Amati violin. It was slightly small for a concert violin, yet its tone was strong and very sweet. It had been made in Italy in 1636, and was original except, possibly, for the pegs and the scroll at the end of the neck.

The Amati brothers were the foremost violin makers in Italy in their time. They had trained Antonio Stradivari and later Giuseppe Guarneri in their shop. These two families took the art of violin making to its pinnacle, but their teachers, the Amatis, certainly produced many of the finest instruments we have today.

The music school was eventually moved out of the house and into its own building at Haverford and Harvard Avenues. Margaret was the director of the school and Ruth was head of the violin department. A twenty-page brochure described the school to prospective students and their parents.

A music kindergarten for children between the ages

of three and seven was taught by Elizabeth Hubbard Bonsall. She taught rhythm, note finding, time values, scales, and a bit of technique. Songs, stories, exercises, marching, pictures, and diminutive orchestral instruments were her teaching tools.

Other faculty members included Abby R. Keeley, voice, William A. Schmidt and later Michel Penha, cello, and William M. Kincaid, flute. These men and women were members of the Philadelphia Symphony Orchestra, which was led at the time by the famed Leopold Stokowski. There were also five assistant piano teachers and one assistant in violin, as well as a full-time secretary.

All of the teachers had studied under very fine musicians, and were well-qualified instructors. Abby Keeley went on to teach at the Julliard School of Music. Both Margaret and Ruth had studied music theory under Ralph Kinder, and Margaret had passed the examinations necessary to become a member of The American Guild of Organists, earning the A.G.O. degree. Ruth had studied violin under Sol Marcosson, and Thaddeus Rich, concert master of the Philadelphia Symphony Orchestra, with advanced work under Theodore Spiering.

While the music soared, the war raged. World War I had taken many of the young men away from Swarthmore, including Gordon Munce, who had been sent to the French front to fight the Germans. Some of Margaret's suitors were also overseas and near the front lines. So Grace, Grandmother Livingston, and the two girls prayed each day for many of the young men who had been part of the high school and college crowd that had so often come to the house to visit, to ask advice, or to play tennis in the backyard.

Grace was very concerned with the war effort and was often interviewed on her opinions about the war. One interview appeared on December 21, 1918, and was headlined in large capital letters: "WE NEED TO GET NEAR TO GOD AND HEAR HIS 'GO AND SIN NO MORE'!" The article quoted her as saying:

More than any other thing, this war has shown up sin! The sin of the whole world! When the horror and the suffering came, we saw how we had forgotten God and fallen into sins, both personal and national. Sins of intemperance, impurity, Sabbath desecration, selfishness, gain-getting, and most of all, forgetting, ignoring, discrediting God! As our desperation increased, we made wild attempts to reform; and then, while the lists of our beloved dead began to come in, at last we crept near to God, appointing a daily tryst to call upon His name.

God has heard and answered richly! But now, as the Christmas peace rings out, we should hear clearly, distinctly, above the triumphant strains of the voice of victory, the voice of Jesus who said long ago, "Sin no more, lest a worse thing come unto thee!"

Our boys are coming home after having fought death and hell. Many of them have caught a vision of God over there amid the horrors of the battle. When they come back with the "light in their eyes" which we hear so much about, shall they find no answering, understanding light in our eyes, showing that we have had a vision too? We need to get near to God and hear His, "Go, and sin no more"!

Grace was very moved by the suffering and the heartbreak caused by war. She saw it, perhaps in its simplest form, as man's greed for power and for riches. Because of her great concern, many of her books during both World War I and World War II were written about those times in world history. Her concern can be discerned in books such as *Silver Wings, The Red Signal,* and *Big Blue Soldier.* She also wrote her only major nonfiction work after World War I. It was entitled *The War Romance of the Salvation Army,* and was coauthored with Evangeline Booth. The book, with more than 350 pages, had thirty illustrations documenting the role of the Salvation Army in France during World War I. It was published by J. B. Lippincott, Grace's regular publisher.

That year, Grace also produced four novels: *The Red Signal* told the story of an airplane pilot during World War I. *The Search* appeared soon after, and one reviewer described it as follows:

The author has put into this exciting story a conviction and fervor which lifts far above ordinary fiction.

The "search," which carries John Cameron through the tests of wartime, of unsuccessful love, and the difficulties born of the enmity of his superior officer, wins for him in the end all that he has desired. A fine story of victory, physical and spiritual, interwoven with a delicious love story.

Other books written that prolific year were *Exit Betty* and *Bright Arrows*.

It was a year full of joy to see the young men come back from the war. It was also a year of sadness because several of the young men whom they had come to know and love came back maimed. And a few did not come back at all.

When Gordon learned that his outfit was not scheduled to return home for several months, he stayed in France to finish his last year of college at Toulouse University. He was fluent in French and had been the interpreter for his company while fighting in the trenches opposite the Germans on the French border. He returned home in 1920 after completing his courses. But, like thousands of other veterans, he was unable to find employment. So, Ruth and Gordon decided to wait for marriage until Gordon was able to find a job that could support himself and his bride.

Margaret was interested in a young man named Wendell Walker. Grace realized that it would not be long before she would become a "double mother-in-law."

A NEW NAME

C H A P T E R   X I I

GRACE always had a strong sense of family unity. As an only child, she was close to both parents. And since her aunts, uncles, and cousins usually lived nearby, there was frequent contact with them, sometimes daily. After her father died, there was no question about what her mother would do; Grace took the responsibility for her support, and her mother moved in with her and helped to raise her two girls.

Grace was a strong woman and was the head of her household in every sense. She had a strong desire to keep the family unit intact. In fact, when her daughters grew up and married, Grace wanted the whole family to live with her in the big house on Cornell Avenue.

Ruth, her youngest daughter, was the first to be married. Gordon and his bride rented a house a few miles away, despite much protest from Grace. However, her mother and Margaret were still at home, so she was not alone in the house. The following year, Ruth became ill and needed nursing care. At Grace's urging, Gordon and Ruth moved back into the house at Swarthmore. That same year Grace's mother passed away. The following year, Margaret married Wendell Walker, and both of Grace's newly married daughters and their husbands lived in her home.

This arrangement worked out reasonably well. But after about two years, the Walkers decided to move into a house of their own. The girls owned the house that had housed their music school, which had been closed a short time earlier. The young couples decided that the Walkers could make some alterations and move into the house at Haverford and Harvard Avenues. Grace opposed the move and, in fact, tried to stop it in every way she could. She argued that it was breaking up the family. When that was not accepted, she reasoned that, having been a good mother and a helpful mother-in-law, this was a great insult and showed a lack of loyalty. Wendell and Margaret, however, had made their decision. The day they started to move their things to the other house, Grace really seemed to panic. Actually, she threw a tantrum. She was hysterical, and nothing the family could do could calm her down. Eventually, she wore herself out and managed to pull herself together.

It was an especially severe blow to Grace to feel that she was losing close touch with Margaret, her firstborn.

Grace had depended heavily on Margaret for close fellowship ever since her husband and father had died, and then when Mr. Lutz had disappointed her. Margaret was staunch and loyal. No doubt Grace's own actions embarrassed her, and when she saw that the Walkers were going to go no matter what she said or did, she did not further oppose the move.

It took a while for Grace to reestablish comfortable relationships with Margaret and Wendell, but within a short time family members were friendly and congenial with each other again. After all, the Walkers were only a short distance away and came often to visit.

Grace and Gordon had great affection for each other and, in fact, had unusually good rapport. Although Ruth wished to have her own home also, Gordon felt strongly that Grace needed them and it would be best for all members of the family if they continued to live with her. So the Munces stayed in the big house on Cornell Avenue for a number of years. Grace was still a highly productive author, yet she was getting on in years. So it was a great help to have family close by.

In the early 1930s, the Walkers took an assignment with the Home Mission Board of the Southern Presbyterian Church to do home mission work in the rural areas of Kentucky. Again, Grace strongly opposed their leaving the area completely; but the Walkers, feeling that God had called them to this ministry, moved into the rural setting of the Kentucky mountains. Eventually, Grace realized that the Walkers were being used of God in church ministry and youth work—the very things in which she was interested—and that, at least in part, it was an outreach from her own ministry of helping her children to put spiritual values and the care of others as important priorities in their lives. Once Grace saw the move in perspective, she was proud of Margaret and Wendell and talked lovingly of them; she anticipated their visits back to her home where she eagerly greeted them and never again opposed their desire for Christian service.

After several years, Gordon, who worked for a large oil company, was transferred to Virginia. This time Grace did not react as she had when the Walkers left; she had learned that, in all things, she must put her trust in God. Even that dearest of earthly things—her family—was in God's hands, and she need not worry about them or about herself.

The transfer was to be for only two years. As God would have it, Allyn Walker, the son of Margaret and Wendell, was now college age, and had come to live with Grace during his last two college years. This was a wonderful provision from the Lord, and Grace was thrilled to have him with her while the Munces were away.

Allyn was an unusually bright young man who could do a variety of things very well. He was not only a good student, but an accomplished musician, both on piano and organ. He also had a bent for mechanical things.

He learned that a church was being torn down to

make way for a new building. Not long before the wrecking crew was to begin knocking down the exterior walls, Allyn walked in to look around. He found a magnificent pipe organ and got permission to remove it before the building was destroyed. Within a short time, that entire large pipe organ was delivered to the Hill house via a large dump truck and Allyn took it, piece by piece, into the basement.

Allyn put the pipe organ back together again and had it working within a few months. He often went down into that dungeon and played that enormous pipe organ by the hour. The floors trembled when Allyn was playing at his best!

About the time that Allyn was graduated from college, the Munces moved back to Swarthmore, so once again Grace had family living with her. They stayed with Grace for the rest of her life.

Grace had a tremendous influence on her family, including her grandchildren. Margaret had two children: Allyn, who became a pastor, and Marcia, who spent many years serving God with her husband in Taiwan. Gordon and Ruth adopted two children. The first, Gordon, became an accountant and was active in his local church, and I, Robert, was the second. I was a missionary in Africa for a number of years, then developed a Christian literature distribution system to supply inexpensive Bibles and Christian books to the poorer countries of the world.

As Grace's youngest grandson, I lived in the Swarthmore house during the last few years of her life. I was quite a young boy when I lived in the big stone house on Cornell Avenue, and my grandmother was quite an elderly lady. I remember incidents, rather than long periods of time. One incident I recall clearly occurred on my fourth birthday. The entire family gathered in the dining room for my birthday party. My grandmother sat at one end of the table and my father at the head of the table. My brother and I were seated on each side of my mother; across the table from us was my cousin Allyn. It was an exciting time, with presents from each member of the family, and lots of cake and ice cream. My grandmother sat there, quietly enjoying the party. Then she said, "Allyn, why don't you give Bobby your present now."

It was no surprise to the family when Cousin Allyn came up with an original idea for giving me my present. He had worked out a treasure hunt that was laid out all over the house. Since I was not yet able to read, I had to find each clue and bring it back to the dining room for somebody to read it to me so I could find the next clue. To retrieve the final clue, I had to go to the top of the third-floor stairs. It was a spooky place for a four year old. I walked up the stairs to the second floor where our bedrooms were, through the sitting room, turned the corner, opened the door to the third-floor staircase, and stood at the bottom listening. The silence was terrible! Then I heard a gentle *thump, thump, thump,* like footsteps. I didn't realize the sound was merely the blood pumping past my own eardrums. It sounded like the footsteps of a monster to me, and I had visions of something like a rhinoceros slowly coming toward me.

The staircase to the third floor had high sides, and all I could see were the white walls and the natural wood steps. How I wanted to run back down those steps and join the others in the dining room; but I had to get that last clue to find my present. Then I started to tiptoe up the stairs. When I got within an arm's reach of the last step, I reached up, snatched the note, and ran full speed all the way down the stairs. When I got back to the dining room I was breathless, but I had that last clue.

Everyone was smiling at me as I came into the room, and I wasn't sure why. But my grandmother put her arm around me, gave me a squeeze and a kiss, and said that she was happy I was having such a wonderful birthday. That calmed me and my pulse was soon back to normal. I was a bit angry, though, when I discovered that my present had been hidden under the dining room table all the time. It was a beautiful large toy sailboat with a wooden hull and real canvas sails. It was certainly one of the nicest presents I have ever received.

That birthday party was typical of the love and fellowship that was experienced in our home.

As a child, I often went into my grandmother's room and watched her write. She sat at her desk and typed on an open-sided typewriter. Even in her old age she typed very fast, and I watched the words being formed on the paper. She only worked a few minutes at a time in those days, and then someone helped her to her bed, or to the daybed under the window. She rested or napped until she had the energy to get up and continue her work.

One of the first heartaches I can remember was caused by a remark by my grandmother. I wandered into her room just as my mother was helping her to the bed. My mother was holding her by one arm, and Grandmother looked at me and asked, "Who is that little boy?" in a tone that sounded as if she didn't really want me there. I loved my grandmother very much and was very hurt that she didn't recognize me.

She was a remarkable woman: she was dying, her body was wearing out, she had cancer, and yet when she had the strength to get out of bed and sit at her typewriter, her memory, which was failing, came back in a flood. She picked up her writing right where she left off, and continued with the story for a page or two, until she ran out of energy. Then her memory would lapse, her body would sag, and she would ask for help to get back to the bed. In those rare moments when she was ready to write, she was also ready to acknowledge the people around her. Her mind was sharp and she would recognize each of us.

None of the grandchildren ever called her "grandmother." We certainly never called her by her first name. We called her "Baba," the name Allyn, her first grandchild, gave to her before he could really talk. The name stuck.

Over the years, Grandmother had tremendous influence upon me. At the earliest age I can remember, the love, reverence, and respect we all had for her was generated by her work ethic which made her so productive, while still fulfilling her responsibilities to God and her family. Her unbounded energy was infectious and made even the youngest of us want to perform at our highest levels. But far more valuable was the underlying peace that was instilled in us, because we all learned early that the Lord Jesus should be sovereign in our lives.

There are many things in life which we cannot explain. One of them is how God, in his sovereignty, chooses who will be our parents. As a child rejected by both natural parents, for whatever reason, and handed over to an adoption agency, it may seem that I had a very poor start in this world. Yet a miracle of God's grace took place in my life at the age of two weeks, when two Christian people came to the agency and chose me, above other children, to be their son. I became the son of Gordon and Ruth Munce, and also the grandson of Grace Livingston Hill.

Natural children, under our legal system, can be written out of a will and rejected by their parents, even in later life. But adopted children can never be written out of a will. Jesus tells us that: "Ye have not chosen me, but I have chosen you, and ordained you, that ye should go and bring forth fruit, and that your fruit should remain: that whatsoever ye shall ask of the Father in my name, he may give it you" (John 15:16, KJV).

Because I was adopted into the Munce family, I was led to an understanding of how to be adopted into God's spiritual family. Therefore, I owe both my physical and spiritual well-being to the adoption process. Perhaps this is my best opportunity to say, "Thank you for your faithfulness to God," to Grace Livingston Hill and to my family, and to thank God for His unmerited favor toward me. My first gift in life was a new birth certificate and on it a new name was written.

CHANCE OF A LIFETIME

CHAPTER XIII

GRACE was involved in four churches during her time in Swarthmore. They were the Swarthmore Presbyterian Church, the Third Presbyterian Church in Chester, Pennsylvania, the Leiperville Church in Leiperville, and the Blue Church on Baltimore Pike, on Route 1, which passes through Swarthmore on its way to Philadelphia.

Grace involved herself and her children in the Swarthmore Presbyterian Church immediately following her move into the house she rented just after her husband died. She taught the Junior classes in the Sunday school and directed the Christian Endeavor Society. Later, both of her daughters were involved in Sunday school teaching and in the music of the church. Margaret often played the organ at the eleven o'clock worship service.

Sunday evening vespers were held at five o'clock, preceded by about fifteen minutes of organ music. In addition to the Bible message, there was often some special music during the vesper hour. Occasionally, in her teen years, Ruth played violin solos at Vespers. Following the service, various committees met. The missionary society often met to discuss the work for the Italians at the Fairview Church, also known as the Leiperville Church.

The church at Leiperville had originally been a country church, officially known as the Ridley Church. In June of 1900, the name was changed to Leiper Church. The church was started in a rural setting, serving mostly the local farm community, then found itself in a more urban setting as the immigrant Italian community grew up around it.

Church attendance dwindled so much that the presbytery did not assign a pastor to the small congregation. Those who were interested moved their memberships to churches in Swarthmore or other nearby towns. The old stone church, with its graveyard beside it, sat empty for many Sundays. Very slowly the church began to deteriorate. The stone structure with its slate roof withstood the elements quite well. The interior furnishings were sturdy and austere, with unpadded, hard wooden benches and plain, plastered walls. The church was not dead, but it slept for a number of years. Grace had a part in its awakening.

One day when she was having some additions made to her house, one of the Italian stonemasons asked if she and her daughters would put on a little concert for the Italian community in Avondale, near Wallingford, about two miles down the road. The date was set for the following Sunday afternoon.

The unpaved roads were a little bit muddy as the magnificent 1924 Lincoln touring car pulled up in front of their host's house on the outskirts of the little community. Immediately the car was surrounded by dozens of charming but dirty children, who talked excitedly about the splendid automobile with its shiny gray paint and matching gray interior.

When the stonemason and his family had piled into the back seat with Grace, Margaret drove them to a small, open field where a crowd of more than two hundred people awaited them. The girls performed flute and violin pieces, all by classic Italian composers. The audience loudly applauded and cheered after each number.

Following the concert, Grace gave a short talk, and asked the parents if they would be willing to let her come and teach a Sunday school class for their children each Sunday afternoon. The response was overwhelming, and a date was set to start within three weeks.

Grace rented an upstairs room in an empty shop in Avondale for the Sunday school. She admired the hard-working people in the neighborhood, most of whom were stonemasons. They were good craftsmen, but their pay was low; because of their lack of English, people often took advantage of them.

The Italians lived in Avondale as peasants in Italy had lived for hundreds of years in the old country. On hot summer days, it wasn't unusual to see the women sitting outside their tiny bungalows (they were little more than shacks), naked from the waist up, nursing their children. The young man who occasionally helped Grace with the Sunday school told her of visiting one home to invite the children to Sunday school. With a twinkle in his eye, he told Grace, "And the child's mother was 'in her own raiment clad'!"

If the people were primitive by suburban Philadelphia standards, it didn't matter very much to Grace. She did not think of herself as being any better than those people to whom she was ministering. She realized that she had had the advantage of education, a bit of money, and a society in which her language, English, was spoken.

Few of the children were ready for Sunday school when the teacher arrived; but as soon as the car appeared, mothers ran out and shouted at their children to get ready for Sunday school. Often the children arrived with a clean dress or shirt pulled over the dirty one that they had been playing in. Faces might be covered with dirt, and cheeks smeared with mustard which had oozed from sandwiches gulped down quickly. But the shirt or dress on the outside was clean. Grace used to say that is probably the way we all look to God, trying to cover our sin and our guilt with an inadequate facade. In the wintertime, some children came to class sewed into woolen suits, which would not be removed until spring.

Grace tried to accept any hospitality that the people offered, but it was often difficult to cross over the strong cultural boundaries. Occasionally she and her group turned down food and drink, and at times this offended the people who were trying to be kind. The Italians had difficulty understanding why their friends consistently refused the wine they offered.

There may have been reasons for the refusal which were less high-principled than temperance societies advocated! One Sunday afternoon a group of six or seven stonemasons returned home from work about the time Sunday school was being dismissed. They invited the teachers to watch them crush grapes. The men removed their work shoes, climbed into the wooden vat filled with grapes, and began to dance around. No one bothered to wash his feet before jumping into the fruit-filled vat. Before long the juice rose in the vat, and people filled their tin cups and joyfully drank the fresh grape juice. Grace and the girls politely declined their shares. Obviously feelings were hurt, but it was a cultural hurdle that they were unable to bridge.

The Sunday school had expanded, with many of the faithful attenders coming from the Leiperville area, about three miles distant. Several of the men asked

Grace if she would be willing to move the Sunday school to Leiperville. They suggested that the old Presbyterian church there would be a good place to meet. They pointed out that the church had been closed for several years and that Grace, being prominent in the Swarthmore Presbyterian Church, could easily get permission to meet there. Indeed, she had no difficulty in getting permission to use the old building because it had been a mission church of the Swarthmore church. She was assisted by the pastor, Dr. Tuttle, and by Mr. Charles Garrett, who was the treasurer of the Swarthmore church.

A number of people helped with the Leiperville work. The Sunday school started immediately with a large number of children and grown-ups. The elders of the Swarthmore Presbyterian Church directed the Italian Mission at Fairview. They took responsibility for the church's financial affairs, and helped recruit Sunday school teachers and other workers. Grace was always there, ready to assist in any way that she could. Eventually there were four teachers: Grace taught the adult class, Mrs. Fisher the young boys, Mrs. Hardcastle the young girls, and Miss Hardcastle the little ones. Music was provided by Margaret and Ruth. Mrs. Hardcastle always brought flowers and made attractive arrangements for the front of the church.

Other helpful activities were started at the church. English classes were taught on Monday evenings, and Grace led a prayer meeting every Tuesday night. Later, when the English classes were discontinued, the prayer meeting was moved to Monday evenings. Within a short time, the prayer meeting became more of a Bible study time. Grace contacted a young pastor, William Allan Dean, to teach the Bible study. The Bible study class was held for nearly twelve years.

Of the thirty to forty people who showed up regularly, only three or four of them came from the Italian community. There were two reasons for the low attendance by the Italians: one, they had difficulty understanding English, and two, they often worked late into the evenings. So the ministry had been expanded and was not only a Sunday school for the Italian community, but reached out to people of other ethnic backgrounds during Bible study time.

One who regularly attended that Sunday school remembers that when he was a young boy, "Mrs. Hill was a very elderly woman. She would sit quietly, obviously happy to be there, but taking no visibly active part in the church," he recalls. But Grace still maintained the role of benefactor and paid the bills of the little church whenever there was a shortfall in finances. In fact, right from the start she took such an interest in the Italian community that if she heard that someone was sick, she sent her car around to take the patient to the hospital or to a doctor. Then she paid the bill. Grace never learned to drive, so she sent her son-in-law or anyone else who could handle the car to run these errands for her.

The spirit of her concern for the people of the community spilled over into the little Sunday school group itself. Minutes of the Leiperville Church show that money was given to two families who could not afford to buy coal during the winter. Although the collections were small and the people were poor, Grace's example showed them their responsibility to reach out in Christian love to others.

The church members reached out to their beloved benefactor, too. When they heard that Grace's mother had her ninetieth birthday, the entire Sunday school bought flowers, signed a greeting card, and sent them to her.

The Swarthmore church also took responsibility for the maintenance of the church building. A letter from the secretary of the trustees of that church shows their concern for the ministry of Leiperville:

At the last regular meeting of the Session, a motion was unanimously adopted instructing the Clerk of the Session to address a letter to the Board of Trustees, asking them to make as early arrangement as seems to them possible for repairing the plastering in the church room at Fairview.

The plaster has fallen or crumbled away at a number of places; in one place, several square yards and the furring with it have come off bodily. This is high from the floor, where the repair work cannot be done by the men of the church. The Italians have *given performances in the church to raise funds for the painting and renovation of the room, which they cannot carry out until the plaster is repaired. They have in the neighborhood of $35.00 in this fund, and some months ago had unbounded enthusiasm for going ahead with the work, but as the months pass without action, they are losing that enthusiasm, not only for the repair work, but for the services in the dilapidated surroundings, and our work is gradually losing in effectiveness, not entirely from this reason, but partly so.*

The Session would urge that this matter have the prompt attention of the Board of Trustees.

After that meeting, the church was soon repaired, and a group from the Italian community redecorated the church. The walls were painted white, and a motto was mounted over the pulpit that read, "The Joy of the Lord Is Your Strength." A few colored pictures were hung on the walls; one depicting the Good Shepherd was the most prominent.

Although the church was very plain, it had a marvelous grand piano, which had served well for many years and still had a beautiful tone. The building was always spotless and clean. The yard was always cut, and the grass was trimmed around the old gravestones. This work was lovingly done by two men who came regularly to Grace's Sunday school class. Santino ("Sunday") DiMateo and his friend Dominic worked together to keep the grounds looking their best. They took special pride in keeping the church library in order, with its many inspirational books which had been donated by members of the Swarthmore church.

Grace's loving involvement with the Leiperville Church and the Italian community lasted for more than 25 years and ended only when she went home to be with the Lord she served.

HOMING

CHAPTER XIV

RUTH, Grace's younger daughter, reminisces about life with the well-known author, and her influence on both her daughters and other young people.

Mother was very family oriented all her life, and it shows in all of her books. As an individual she was original, full of humor, and very artistic. She had a tremendous admiration of anyone who was well-educated and successful, almost to the point of being in awe of them. She was also very friendly and helpful, always ready to drop what she was doing to help when there was a need. As a pastor's wife, she was certainly helpful to my father.

I remember Mother as being very strict in her discipline. Yet whenever there was need for punishment, she always made sure we understood why it was necessary.

When I was about five years old, my mother bought me a little bike, the smallest size she could get. We were living in Swarthmore then, just three years after my father died. I was thrilled to receive such a wonderful gift, and I quickly learned to ride.

There was a little terrace in front of the house, about three feet high. The top of the terrace was only about twenty-five or thirty feet from the street. I liked to ride down the slant of the terrace toward the street. Mother saw me do this one day and told me not to do it again because she could see that the momentum carried me into the street. Even then there were some automobiles and certainly many horse-drawn wagons and trucks. Mother severely reprimanded me, then went into the house to prepare for the picnic she had planned for us that afternoon.

The second time I got caught, she said, "If you do that again you can't go to the picnic with us." But, as soon as she went into the house and I thought she wasn't looking, down the terrace I went. I was still young enough to sleep in a crib, and that is where she put me and where I stayed, weeping my heart out, while the others were picnicking. Mrs. Morton, an apple-cheeked little Scotswoman whom we loved, stayed with me until I cried myself to sleep. When the family returned home, my mother explained that

*what she said must be obeyed. It was a good lesson;
I learned that you obey or else!*

*In retrospect, I consider Mother to have been a
very good disciplinarian. Never did my sister or I
doubt her love for us. When something had to be
taken away, she always made it up to us in some
other way.*

*As we grew older, Mother was extremely helpful in
answering our questions. When sex questions came
up, she always answered straightforwardly and
plainly so we could understand. She only went as far
as we asked, and then dropped it. But she gave us a
very beautiful, loving, and understandable view of
sex. Consequently, when it came time for dating, we
understood why "petting" was not the right thing to
do, and what caused difficulties in the lives of young
people who went too far.*

*As a mother of two young daughters, she was
strict in regulating our friendships. I resented this
when I was young, but as I grew older, I was grateful for it. We had plenty of fun, and had many
friends. As we went into our teen years, she turned
the whole backyard into a clay tennis court. All of
the young people of the neighborhood came to enjoy
tennis games with us.*

*There were four churches in town when we moved
there. None of them really taught the Bible very
much. They were more like social clubs. We settled*

on one of them whose pastor was a very delightful
and friendly man. We discovered later that he did
not know the basic Christian view of salvation.

Despite the impoverished spiritual condition of the
church, Mother began to take an interest in Sunday
school and youth work. Margaret and I were taken
to Sunday school, of course, as soon as we could be
taken out of the house. We were taught to sit quietly
throughout the church service. When the sermons
were boring, my sister and I exercised our newly ac-
quired math skills by taking the square root of the
numbers on the hymnal board, or turning them into
some kind of mathematical equation. At least we
learned to sit quietly and appreciate the fact that
here was a group of Christian people gathered
together to learn more about God. There wasn't
much learning, but we did absorb something.

Mother soon had charge of the junior department
in Sunday school. Then she started a Junior Christian Endeavor Society. She became interested in
starting a group through her contacts with Amos R.
Wells, well-known editor of the Christian Endeavor
World. She made sure we got good Bible teaching in
our meetings.

It was in those meetings that the youth of our
church learned to pray aloud in what they called
sentence prayers, very short heartfelt expressions.
There were also opportunities to give brief testi-
monies of what the Lord had done for us during the

*week, or to tell how prayers had been answered. We
learned to pray with our friends, and we learned to
ask them to pray for us and our problems. We also
memorized much Scripture.*

*Along with the spiritual side of Christian Endeavor,
we had a lot of fun together. On hiking trips there
were opportunities for counseling and discussing our
problems. The activities of the church became, for
most of us, the center of our lives. Our C. E. group
grew to nearly one hundred young people, from ages
eight to eighteen. The Christian Endeavor Society
provided our main social event each week, with pic-
nics, games, music, and counseling. We had good
schools in Swarthmore and they taught us important
facts, but C. E. showed us how to live.*

*Mr. Lutz left just before I graduated from high
school in 1914. His departure ended a lot of unhappiness in our home. My older sister Margaret took over
the music school, and I assisted her. Both of us had
been involved since our early teens. Some parents
could not make their children practice music, so they
sent them to me. I earned a quarter for overseeing
their practice for an hour. It was my mother's idea.
She was, as always, the moving spirit behind initiating new things.*

*I learned a lot about teaching and making children
like what they were doing. I learned this, of course,
from her. When any work had to be done, Mother
always made a game of it, or a competition to see*

who could do it best, or finish first. She made work exciting and fun, rather than just plodding through ordinary tasks.

Through the music school, Mother formed a Swarthmore Choral Society. This began some years before my stepfather left.

The music school started in our home and, at one time, we had five pianos in the house. One of them was hoisted up to the third floor by a crane. There was always music in our home.

Another of my mother's ideas was that a regular oratorio should be learned by the young people. "Naaman" was chosen and the parts were given out and learned. We performed this in costume at the Swarthmore Women's Club. It was a great success. We also gave it at the Steel Pier in Atlantic City, and at many churches. I doubt that any of the young people in that group ever forgot the story of Naaman, which shows the marvelous power of God in healing. The very words of Scripture were repeated throughout the oratorio and I'm sure this had an effect on their Christian faith.

All of the activities developed for youth by my mother show that she was continually thinking of new, original, and educational training for us. She always urged the young people around her to work toward their very best—to make the most of the abilities they were born with. It is easy to see why so many of her stories show a young girl left penniless, without friends, and having to make it on her own, and why her heroines were forced to use their own ingenuity to make something, do something, or go somewhere. The heroines in her books were usually fond of their parents, and the father was often the hero figure.

My mother had been grounded in her youth in God's way of saving souls, and she and her mother taught Margaret and me very faithfully the Word of God. As soon as we could talk, my grandmother, Marcia Livingston, taught us Bible stories and drilled us in memorizing Psalms and other Bible verses, even whole chapters of the Bible. We continued to read the Bible aloud each day, just as we had when my father was alive. By the time we finished school, we were probably better grounded in the truths of the Bible than most young people were.

One of the fellows who had been in the Christian Endeavor Society entered college the same year I did. He was the one who taught me to throw a ball like a boy and paddle a canoe. We were very fond of each other, and much later we married. He was very popular among the students. He joined a good frater- nity and brought his friends to our house often.

Most of the fraternity boys used our house as a second home, and had special counseling from my mother when they needed it. Her counseling shows up in her books, especially in The Witness, *which was one of her most popular books. John*

Wanamaker was so taken with this book that he gave away thousands of copies to employees and friends. He even did a full window display of it in his prestigious department store. Francis Schaeffer, the late well-known Christian writer and founder of L'Abri, was helped by this book in his youth, according to a quote in his wife's book, The Tapestry.

Some of our college friends led Margaret and me on escapades which made my mother uneasy. One day, we climbed to the top of the water tank behind the college, which was a risky thing to do. We saw the Delaware River, three or four miles away, and had a commanding view of the whole area. When we told Mother where we had been, she shook from fright! But when we told her what a wonderful view we had from the top she didn't scold, but heaved a sigh of relief that we were safe. She let the fellows know that she trusted them to take care of her girls, and they never violated that trust.

Mother took part in many of our activities, yet she was also writing two or three novels a year, averaging 80,000 words each. She certainly got the most out of each day—and night, for she often wrote until 2:00 or 3:00 A.M. "when the house was quiet."

Because the young people came to our house so often, there was always extra cooking and housework. Mother had a very efficient all-around helper, Gladys Quinlan, who was the daughter of a woman who had worked for us some years before. Her father, our church janitor, was a fine man, a national from Jamaica. They were a Christian family and very sympathetic with all the activity going on in our house. Gladys was always ready for the inrush of ravenous fellows, and she made the world's best maple cakes! She enjoyed the activities and felt she was part of the ministry to the youth of Swarthmore.

About the time we were in college, a neighbor invited Mother to a Bible study in her home. She wasn't well acquainted with the woman, but thought it would be good to go to the class, since she had been invited.

She came home on cloud nine! She heard things she had never heard in church, even from her father or husband. The Bible was opened in such a way that most pastors must have missed in seminary. This "deeper" teaching of Scripture was started about 1850 in England, Ireland, and Wales, as students of God's Word got together and dug out truths from the Bible that had been lost during the Middle Ages. Mrs. Burnette Brooke, the visiting teacher, was the mother of one of our college friends. She taught from the Gospel of John, showing the seven miracles or signs that prove that Jesus is the Son of God. Mother was so enthusiastic about what she had heard, she asked Mrs. Brooke to start a weekly Bible study at our house. Later, when she moved away, Dr. Frank Lange, of Philadelphia Bible College, took the class.

These Bible studies did three things for Mother. She grew in the Word as she had never grown before. They introduced her to other excellent Bible teachers who helped in her future ministries, and they developed her sense of responsibility to God and to people. And they motivated her to start a Sunday school in an immigrant Italian settlement nearby.

A PERSONAL INFLUENCE

CHAPTER XV

GRACE Livingston Hill made a lasting impact on the lives of many young people. She was particularly interested in helping young men and women who, she thought, might develop into full-time Christian workers.

One young man who was influenced by her ministry was Dwight Pentecost, who later became a professor at Dallas Theological Seminary. He has authored eighteen books, including his classic work, *Things to Come*, a systematic summary of Bible prophecies.

The first novels Dwight Pentecost read, apart from those assigned for English classes, were the novels of Grace Livingston Hill. It wasn't until he had read many of her books that he learned that the woman who customarily sat two pews behind his family at the Third Presbyterian Church was the author. He was overawed to be in her presence because of her wide popularity. "But even though I was a young teenager," he says, "she spoke to me, called me by name, and showed a personal interest in me which soon caused me to lose my fear."

Mrs. Hill was always distinguished by the hats she wore, Dwight Pentecost recalls. She was easily recognized from across the church by her extremely large hats. One Sunday the Pentecost family heard someone exclaim, "Oh, my goodness!" as she walked up the aisle. After the service, Mrs. Pentecost turned around. "Do you know what I did?" Mrs. Hill asked. "I put on the wrong hat for this outfit!" Mrs. Hill had a different hat for every outfit, and the color of the hat or flower matched her dress. This time they certainly didn't match.

Dr. Pentecost recalls how Grace Livingston Hill not only had a positive influence on him as a teenager, but also helped set the course of his life.

When I was in high school, Mrs. Hill's daughter, Ruth Munce, was my Sunday school teacher and also my teacher in vacation Bible school. The vacation Bible school movement began in that church, for our pastor was concerned about biblical illiteracy among the young people. He instituted a five-week summer course to teach us the Bible. Later, I was in classes taught by Mrs. Hill's older daughter, Margaret, and her husband, Wendell Walker.

During our high school years, we were frequently invited to Mrs. Hill's home for some of our Sunday school activities. I remember how awed I was on my first visit to her home. It was not an ordinary home; it was one of the most magnificent homes I had ever been in. I had not been used to such handsome furnishings as hand-carved wooden chairs and beautiful Oriental carpets. The large carpet in the living room was so fine, I wondered if I was allowed to walk on it. I remember sitting there and staring at the carpet and admiring its beautiful colors and pattern as we talked. But Mrs. Hill made us all feel perfectly comfortable sitting down in her beautiful living room.

Most boys admire fine cars, and Mrs. Hill's car was one of the finest I have ever seen. The first time I went to her home with the youth group, her beautiful car was standing out in the side yard. I am sure it was parked there just so we could sit behind the wheel! It was a magnificent open Lincoln touring car, equipped with a custom body, and painted a kind of gray-beige. The leather seats were tucked and pleated and matched the color of the car's exterior. I still remember that gray-beige color and would like to have my own car painted the same color. I thought Mrs. Hill's car was the most elegant thing a person could own.

In 1934 and 1935, when I was in high school, I was introduced to a Bible class at the Leiperville Church. I discovered that Mrs. Hill was burdened for

the area because there was no Bible-teaching church
there. She had obtained the use of the church
building and had asked William Allan Dean to teach
on Monday nights. Mrs. Hill was always there and
warmly welcomed those who came for the studies.
During that period, I came to know her, and those
contacts at the Leiperville Church probably led me to
accept her counsel and advice concerning seminary a
few years later.

I went away to college, anticipating preparing for
seminary and entering the pastoral ministry. In
August 1937, before I was to enter seminary, I saw
Mrs. Hill at church. She asked what school I planned
to attend. At that point, I did not know. Three op-
tions were open to me. One of the men in the church
offered to pay all of my expenses at Princeton
Seminary. But the seminary had taken a turn to the
left, which was contrary to all the instruction I had
had in that church. I considered attending either
Westminster Seminary, where my friend Francis
Schaeffer urged me to go, or Faith Seminary, a new
seminary which had broken off from Westminster. I
was in a quandary.

Mrs. Hill invited me to her home on the following
Thursday evening. There she introduced me to Rev.
Henry Woll, who had recently graduated from Dallas
Theological Seminary. I had not heard of the school,
although at the Leiperville Church I had heard its
president, Dr. Lewis Sperry Chafer, teach on several

occasions. Mr. Woll talked about the school in Dallas, and told me about the curriculum and its biblical emphasis.

I recalled that Mr. Woll had been a teacher in a summer Bible conference I attended as a teenager. I had been impressed with his ability to expound the Scriptures, and I had wanted to be able to teach the Bible like that myself some day. Now I knew where he had gotten his training.

I told Mrs. Hill I would like to go to the seminary in Dallas. But school was to open in two weeks, and I didn't see how I could apply and be accepted in so short a time. She wrote to Dr. Chafer, the president, and recommended me. He sent a telegram inviting me to come. I received my seminary training there: four years for a Master's program and, later, three additional years for a Doctoral degree. Thus, Mrs. Hill was instrumental in setting the course of my entire ministry.

She continued her interest in me while I was in seminary, even writing to me from time to time. I recall, with gratitude, that two or three times she sent a check for $25 to help with expenses and to show her support. This encouraged me greatly. I believe she helped many other young men in a similar way, which shows something of her character.

MORE THAN CONQUEROR

CHAPTER XVI

OVER the years, Grace was in great demand as a public speaker and, during her lifetime, spoke at hundreds of churches and public conference centers. There were so many speeches to be made that she was unable to prepare an original presentation for each one of them. Her audiences were eager to hear something about her latest book. Because so many people had read the entire series, they were looking forward to whatever would come from her pen. This prompted Grace to put her books into summarized form. In her private library, many of the volumes had pages paper-clipped together and paragraphs crossed out so that the books were condensed to as few as five pages or as many as fifty pages, depending on how long her speech was to last.

At conference centers and sometimes at churches, several speakers or authors were sometimes asked to give five- to fifteen-minute speeches, one right after the other. Thus, in one evening, the listeners got a preview of several new books. Grace was often invited to speak at such meetings, and she was always ready to give a summary of her latest book.

Grace continued her speaking engagements up until the age of 79. After that she didn't have the energy to travel and hold public meetings. Her last public interview was written by James M. Neville of *The Sunday Bulletin* Book Review. It was entitled, "Novelist Emphasizes Happiness Theme in All Stories," and appeared as follows:

Mrs. Grace Livingston Hill, at 81, published her 79th book last month.

Religious inspiration blended with "boy-meets-girl" romance has served Mrs. Grace Livingston Hill as a durable story formula that has survived the literary fads and fashions for more than 50 years.

"WHERE TWO WAYS MEET," her 79th book by J. B. Lippincott, her main publisher, and published last month, deals "with the re-affirmation of a man's faith."

Often termed as one of America's most beloved novelists, as well as the most prolific, Mrs. Hill's books are invariably overlooked by critics and reviewers because of her frankly escapist stories and unvarying happy endings.

Mrs. Hill, however, had a direct answer for this oversight in her Swarthmore home.

"I feel," she said, with sincerity, "that there is enough sadness and sorrow in the world. So I try to end all my books as beautifully as possible, since that is God's way—and the best way."

Just how many millions of faithful readers hold her viewpoint is suggested by the statement of her long-time publishers, J. B. Lippincott & Co., that Mrs. Hill "has more books to her credit than any other writer, living or dead."

Unlike some popular women novelists who sell a million copies with one title, Mrs. Hill's romances hold to a steady 16,000 copies. Her reprint sales are more than double that number, leading the field, according to a recent survey, with a total of 76 titles to date. Each reprint sells 33,000 copies, or more. She publishes three novels a year.

Trailing her for popularity in the reprint field are Zane Grey, 43; Sir Walter Scott, 32; Charles Dickens, 31; and Anthony Trollope, 31.

It is estimated that more than 4,000,000 copies of her novels have been printed in this country alone.

Her ability to hold successive generations as readers, Mrs. Hill explains simply "because I am not writing just for the sake of writing.

"I have attempted to convey, in my own way, and through my novels, a message which God has given, and to convey that message with whatever abilities were given to me."

A highly articulate woman with a deep religious sense which has colored her long and active life, Mrs. Hill said that "whatever I've been able to accomplish has been God's doing. I've tried to follow His teaching in all my writing and thoughts."

The evangelist novelist, who will be 82 years old on April 16, lives in a comfortable three-story stone house on Cornell Avenue, Swarthmore. A second-floor room is set aside as her workshop. She writes directly on the typewriter, and does little rewriting.

"My working hours? I work whenever I can find the time. In more than 50 years I haven't had one real vacation."

Mrs. Hill, who looks much younger than her age, comes from a family of ministers and writers. Her father was Rev. Charles M. Livingston, of Wellsville, N.Y. Her husband, who died seven years after their marriage in 1892, was Rev. Thomas Hill, also a Presbyterian minister, like her father.

In the general scheme of things, her development as an evangelical novelist was natural enough. Besides her religious family background, she had before her two examples of successful authorship. Her mother wrote love stories about the Civil War,

HAPPINESS HILL

HEAD OF THE HOUSE

HOMING

THE HONEYMOON HOUSE

THE HONOR GIRL

HOUSE ACROSS THE HEDGE

IN THE WAY

IN TUNE WITH WEDDING BELLS

JOB'S NIECE

KATHARINE'S YESTERDAY

KERRY

LADYBIRD

A LITTLE SERVANT

LO, MICHAEL

LONE POINT—A SUMMER OUTING

THE LOVE GIFT

THE MAN OF THE DESERT

MARCIA SCHUYLER

MARIGOLD

MARIS

MATCHED PEARLS

MIRANDA

MISS LAVINIA'S CALL

MORE THAN CONQUERER

MYSTERY FLOWERS

THE MYSTERY OF MARY
A NEW NAME
NOT UNDER THE LAW
THE OBSESSION OF VICTORIA GRACEN
OUT OF THE STORM
PANSIES FOR THOUGHTS
THE PARKERSTOWN DELEGATE
PARTNERS
THE PATCH OF BLUE
PATRICIA
A PERSONAL INFLUENCE
PHOEBE DEANE
THE PRODIGAL GIRL
RAINBOW COTTAGE
THE RANSOM
RE-CREATIONS
THE RED SIGNAL
ROSE GALBRAITH
THE SEARCH
THE SEVENTH HOUR
SILVER WINGS
THE SOUND OF THE TRUMPET
THE SPICE BOX
THE STORY OF A WHIM
THE STRANGE PROPOSAL

STRANGER WITHIN THE GATES

THE STREET OF THE CITY

SUBSTITUTE GUEST

SUNRISE

THROUGH THESE FIRES

TIME OF THE SINGING OF BIRDS

TOMORROW ABOUT THIS TIME

THE TRYST

AN UNWILLING GUEST

A VOICE IN THE WILDERNESS

THE WAR ROMANCE OF THE SALVATION ARMY

WHERE TWO WAYS MET

THE WHITE FLOWER

THE WHITE LADY

WHITE ORCHIDS

THE WITNESS

CHRISTIAN HERALD ASSOCIATION AND ITS MINISTRIES

CHRISTIAN HERALD ASSOCIATION, founded in 1878, publishes The Christian Herald Magazine, one of the leading interdenominational religious monthlies in America. Through its wide circulation, it brings inspiring articles and the latest news of religious developments to many families. From the magazine's pages came the initiative for CHRISTIAN HERALD CHILDREN and THE BOWERY MISSION, two individually supported not-for-profit corporations.

CHRISTIAN HERALD CHILDREN, established in 1894, is the name for a unique and dynamic ministry to disadvantaged children, offering hope and opportunities which would not otherwise be available for reasons of poverty and neglect. The goal is to develop each child's potential and to demonstrate Christian compassion and understanding to children in need.

Mont Lawn is a permanent camp located in Bushkill, Pennsylvania. It is the focal point of a ministry which provides a healthful "vacation with a purpose" to children who without it would be confined to the streets of the city. Up to 1000 children between the age of 7 and 11 come to Mont Lawn each year.

Christian Herald Children maintains year-round contact with children by means of a *City Youth Ministry.* Central to its philosophy is the belief that only through sustained relationships and demonstrated concern can individual lives be truly enriched. Special emphasis is on individual guidance, spiritual and family counseling and tutoring. This follow-up ministry to inner-city children culminates for many in financial assistance toward higher education and career counseling.

THE BOWERY MISSION, located at 227 Bowery, New York City, has since 1879 been reaching out to the lost men on the Bowery, offering them what could be their last chance to rebuild their lives. Every man is fed, clothed and ministered to. Countless numbers have entered the 90-day residential rehabilitation program at the Bowery Mission. A concentrated ministry of counseling, medical care, nutrition therapy, Bible study and Gospel services awakens a man to spiritual renewal within himself.

These ministries are supported solely by the voluntary contributions of individuals and by legacies and bequests. Contributions are tax deductible. Checks should be made out either to CHRISTIAN HERALD CHILDREN or to THE BOWERY MISSION.

Administrative Office: 40 Overlook Drive, Chappaqua, New York 10514
Telephone: (914) 769-9000

BRENTWOOD

BRIGHT ARROWS

BY WAY OF THE SILVERTHORNS

THE CHALLENGERS

THE CHANCE OF A LIFETIME

A CHAUTAUQUA IDYL

THE CHRISTMAS BRIDE

THE CITY OF FIRE

THE CLOUDY JEWEL

COMING THROUGH THE RYE

CRIMSON MOUNTAIN

CRIMSON ROSES

A DAILY RATE

DAPHNE DEANE

DAWN OF THE MORNING

DUSKIN

THE ENCHANTED BARN

THE ESSELSTYNES

EXIT BETTY

THE FINDING OF JASPER HOLT

FOUND TREASURE

A GIRL TO COME HOME TO

THE GIRL FROM MONTANA

THE GIRL OF THE WOODS

THE GOLD SHOE

Books by Grace Livingston Hill

ACCORDING TO THE PATTERN
ALL THROUGH THE NIGHT
AMORELLE
THE ANGEL OF HIS PRESENCE
APRIL GOLD
ARIEL CUSTER
ASTRA
AUNT CRETE'S EMANCIPATION
BEAUTY FOR ASHES
BECAUSE OF STEPHEN
THE BELOVED STRANGER
THE BEST MAN
BIG BLUE SOLDIER
BLUE RUIN

and honour, and glory, and blessing," he concluded: "Let us rejoice for her who joins that song today!"

After a few words and prayer by the Rev. Mr. Cressy, the service was concluded.

Many friends wanted to present a memorial to the memory of Mrs. Hill, and they agreed that the memorial should be a useful one. Gifts were given to support a Grace Livingston Hill Memorial Library at the Bible Institute of Pennsylvania, which was located at 15th and Race Streets, Philadelphia. Many famous radio preachers and authors, as well as prominent people in the community, took part in that memorial. In addition to her daughters, the sponsoring committee included some well-known names: Dr. Harry A. Ironside, honorary chairman, Mr. Harry J. Jaeger, general chairman, Dr. Donald Grey Barnhouse, Rev. James Cowee, Rev. Robert A. Cressy, Rev. William Allan Dean, Dr. D. H. Dolman, Mr. C. Stacey Woods, and many others. But the greatest memorials to Grace Livingston Hill are her books, which have reached out and touched the hearts of ten times as many people after death as during her lifetime.

If Grace were here to comment about her own work today, she would probably simply say, "Thank you, Lord, for using me."

A small boy asked his teacher if she had seen the report in the paper of the death of Mrs. Hill, and added, "My mother told me Mrs. Hill was the first person who ever told her about Jesus."

But if she could speak to us this afternoon from the Glory, she would bid us lift our voices in praise of another—she would tell us about Jesus.

Mr. Dean talked about man's unworthiness to receive praise, and quoted several Bible personalities who felt unworthy:

Jacob, who said: "I am not worthy of the least of all the mercies" (Gen. 32:10, KJV); John the Baptist, whom Jesus called the greatest of all the prophets, yet he acknowledged that "one mightier than I cometh, the latchet of whose shoes I am not worthy to unloose" (Luke 3:16, KJV); and the centurian who had great faith, yet felt, "I am not worthy that thou shouldest enter under my roof" (Luke 7:6, KJV).

"All of us, like the prodigal son who came back to God," Mr. Dean said, "can say, 'I am no more worthy to be called thy son' " (Luke 15:21, KJV).

"Only Jesus," he said, "is worthy of praise because He redeemed us and is the rightful king of both heaven and earth." Then, after reading Revelation 5:12, "Saying with a loud voice, Worthy is the Lamb that was slain to receive power, and riches, and wisdom, and strength,

The interview was written a few weeks before Grace Livingston Hill's death, and accompanied her obituary. Many newspapers headlined her death and pointed out that her life spanned from the end of the Civil War to the discovery of the atomic bomb.

The cause of Grace's death was given "as a general breakdown due to her advanced years and to her having worked hard." Her death came as a shock to thousands of people, and cards and letters poured in from around the world.

Grace's funeral service was conducted by William Allan Dean, the pastor who had come faithfully to the Leiperville Church to teach the Monday night Bible study, and by her good friend, Rev. Robert A. Cressy, who had been her secretary when he was a young man.

Her home church, the Third Presbyterian Church in Chester, Pennsylvania, was not large enough to contain the crowd expected for her service, so it was held in Tenth Presbyterian Church in Philadelphia, which was pastored at the time by Dr. Donald Grey Barnhouse. The Reverend Dean's sermon at her funeral was on the subject of being worthy. He said:

Much might be said in praise of Grace Livingston Hill, for millions blessed her for the work which she had performed. They blessed her for her fine writing, they blessed her for her personal ministry to them, and they blessed her for being a friend and a mother.

Robert, 5. Her other daughter is the wife of Rev. Wendell Walker, who conducts a Bible school for the mountain people of Kentucky and West Virginia.

Mrs. Hill, confined to her room by a recent illness, with half of her 80th novel finished, keeps abreast of the news by reading the daily newspapers and many current magazines.

Commenting on modern literature in general, Mrs. Hill said she failed to find as many "really fine" books as were known when she was a girl listening to her father reading aloud to the family in the evening. Mrs. Hill also thinks modern humor has been spoiled by "sordid situations."

It is also her belief that women writers can dominate the best-seller lists because "women have more time to write than men do, at least when they're beginning. Many women writers, of course, are not under pressure of having to earn a living."

Her method of dreaming up plots, she said, is simply by noting some incident around her home, in the street.

"Anything starts me off," she continued. "A few words overheard, or, more subtle still, an expression on a passing face will set me wondering what story lies behind it, and I go on from there.

"But the magic way to get a story going," she concluded, "is simply to sit down at the typewriter and just go ahead."

*and her aunt, Mrs. G. R. Alden, delighted a Victorian
generation with the "Pansy" Books.*

*Mrs. Hill's first novel effort was an extravagant
tale of two forlorn orphans adopted by a rich
woman. She was 10. Her first published novel was
"A CHAUTAUQUA IDYL," in 1887.*

*With two babies to care for as well as support,
Mrs. Hill took to her writing in earnest.*

*In short order, she began selling everything she
wrote. She was, at times, hard-pressed to keep up
her family duties as a mother and still meet publishers' demands.*

*"That's why I refused to consider my career
separate from my daily family life."*

*Maybe the early years of writing stories while her
babies scrambled and babbled at her knees have
made unnecessary in her home the restrictions im-
posed on households of busy authors.*

*"I can't say I shut myself up in a room," explained
Mrs. Hill. "My door is open at all times. The
telephone constantly interrupts, and then I go back to
my writing. Friends drop in on me, or members of
the family hold a conclave in the next room. If I'm
busy, I simply disconnect my mind and keep working."*

*A resident of Swarthmore since 1902, Mrs. Hill
lives with her daughter and son-in-law, Mr. & Mrs.
J. Gordon Munce, and their children, Gordon, 7, and*